# Sweetie-licious Pies
## Eat Pie, Love Life

# LINDA HUNDT

Photography by Kalman & Pabst Photo Group: Clarissa Westmeyer

skirt!

Guilford, Connecticut
An imprint of Globe Pequot Press

skirt!® is an attitude . . . spirited, independent, outspoken, serious, playful and irreverent, sometimes controversial, always passionate.

Copyright © 2013 Linda Hundt
Photography © Clarissa Westmeyer, Kalman & Pabst Photo Group
Food stylist: Laura Goble
Vintage photographs courtesy of the author

skirt!® is an imprint of Globe Pequot Press.
skirt!® is a registered trademark of Morris Publishing Group, LLC, and is used with express permission.

Project editors: Tracee Williams and Julie Marsh
Text design: Sheryl Kober
Layout: Melissa Evarts

Library of Congress Cataloging-in-Publication Data

Hundt, Linda, author.
  Sweetie-licious pies : eat pie, love life! / Linda Hundt ; photographs by Kalman & Pabst Photo Group, Clarissa Westmeyer.
     pages cm
  ISBN 978-0-7627-8752-4
  1. Pies. I. Title.
  TX773.H842 2013
  641.86'52— dc23

                                                        2013022997


Printed in the United States of America

10 9 8 7 6 5 4 3 2 1

To my sweet and loving family, who thankfully and graciously love pie as much as I do!

# CONTENTS

# FOREWORD: Family Traditions

Family traditions create special childhood memories that help to influence, guide, and sustain us all through our lives. Gathering together for the pleasure of sharing a great meal with one another and enjoying family recipes are things that we in our family cherish and still continue. We baked a lot of pies back then and still do—pie has always been our favorite dessert!

My daughter Linda loved to cook at an early age. She is a graduate of Michigan State University, but took a circuitous route to follow her dream and mission of loving people, creating excellent food, baking unbelievably wonderful pies, and honoring traditions.

Linda's charming and nostalgic shop, Sweetie-licious Bakery Café, in DeWitt, Michigan, is a walk back in time to a bakery of yesteryear. I truly love to visit and eat her cooking. She uses many old family recipes and often creates her own new pie varieties, which are works of art. You too will love her cooking. This beautiful cookbook contains her recipes, ones that I know you'll treasure and love to share with your family and friends, just as we do with ours.

Love to you all,

*Joan*

Joan McComb

# INTRODUCTION: My Life's Sweet Mission

I believe a successful and blessed life is one that has been earned, learned, and loved. This cookbook is all about my family and friends and their stories. I've come to learn how living and baking an honorable life made their lives richer and, dare I say, sweeter. This has certainly been true for me. Most of them did not lead glamorous or wealthy lives. They were simple people who believed in faith, love, loyalty, and hard work. Their success was in how they made everybody who touched their lives feel loved through their cooking and baking talents. We too can emulate their giving nature, by making and eating good pie with those we love!

It is no surprise to anyone who knows me that my Easy-Bake Oven was my favorite Christmas gift. I speak of it often, as it inspired my love for baking and creating at an early age. I remember my twin sister and me as six-year-olds, tearing off the Christmas wrap, exposing the box with a picture of a darling little girl playing with her oven. I loved her hair (which I later imitated), her dress, and that she was baking with her own little oven! I was so thankful to Santa for thinking of me.

After that my memories are mostly scattered. I remember that my sister and I baked for my brothers and how much they seemed to like me when the Easy-Bake was out. I remember all five of us kids hovering around the oven while taking impatient turns staring into the tiny window, watching our brownies bake beautifully under the hundred-

watt lightbulb. Our mother cut the brownies into five pieces so we could all get a taste. We were happy despite the small portion, because we'd made it!

Unfortunately, my beloved Easy-Bake was destroyed in a house fire at my parents' home over twenty years ago. My dear husband, well aware of my fondness for my beloved little oven, decided to find me a replica of my own on eBay—a glorious surprise for me one Christmas morning. As I peeled the Christmas paper off my gift and saw the little girl on the box that I hadn't seen in forty years, all the joy and love I'd felt from cooking and baking throughout my life came rushing back. I realized that my mission in life, my dream of changing the world one pie at a time and loving people through

my food, all started from that little oven. Through my darkest moments, cooking and baking soothed me and gave me a purpose.

I know that my gifts, my blessings, my mission, and my love will always fill my life. Sharing the traditions of our foremothers, and our shared passion for homemade food and the provenance of pies, is my vocation, my life's sweet mission.

As the 2011 Crisco 100 Year Anniversary Innovation Award winner, Crisco National Pie Best of Show $5,000 winner, Food Network Pie Challenge winner, holder of sixteen first-place Crisco National Pie ribbons, owner of the nationally known Sweetie-licious Bakery Café, and thousands and thousands of homemade pies later, I want to share what I have learned. What better way than through this unique cookbook?

I am elated to share with you my recipes, the people who inspired me through their food and lovely way of life, and the legacies they left for us all to aspire to.

xoxo

Linda

Linda Hundt

# Flaky Classic Piecrust

1³/₄ cups flour
¹/₄ teaspoon baking powder
¹/₂ teaspoon salt
1 tablespoon sugar
¹/₂ cup Crisco butter-flavored shortening,
   refrigerated, OR
    ¹/₃ cup shortening plus 3 tablespoons
    butter, ice cold and cut into small chunks
5¹/₂ tablespoons ice water

1. Mix all of the above ingredients, except the water, in a stand mixer using the paddle attachment on medium speed swiftly until the crust appears pealike.

2. Carefully sprinkle the ice-cold water in the crust 1 tablespoon at a time, using approximately 5½ tablespoons. Mix with a fork until the dough starts to become moistened and just gathers together.

3. Pat into a disk, wrap, and refrigerate for at least 30 minutes.

4. Roll the crust out on a floured surface and place into a 9-inch pan. Shape and crimp the crust. Crusts don't have to roll out perfectly; just crimp over any imperfections!

5. Freeze.

Butter makes crusts full of flavor, while shortening gives piecrusts their flakiness.

Always use ice-cold water to make your crusts come together. I use ice water, and I use a tablespoon to sprinkle water in the crust to control the amount—my mother's hint! You can always add more water, but you can never fix a crust that has too much water in it, so be very careful when putting water in your crust.

I recommend freezing all piecrusts to ensure the best quality!

# Sweetie-licious Cream Cheese Crust

1/4 cup plus 2 tablespoons butter, softened
3 ounces cream cheese, softened
1 1/4 cups flour
2 teaspoons sugar
1/8 teaspoon salt

1. Mix butter and cream cheese in a stand mixer using the paddle attachment on medium speed until well blended. Add the flour, sugar, and salt; mix just until blended.

2. Pat into a disk, wrap, and refrigerate for at least 30 minutes.

3. Roll out on a floured surface until the dough is round and 11–12 inches wide. Place into a 9-inch pan. Shape and crimp the crust.

4. Freeze.

This crust browns easily, so cover with foil if it becomes too brown!

# Sweetie-licious Graham Cracker Crust

1 1/2 cups crushed graham crackers
3 tablespoons sugar
1/8 teaspoon salt
1/3 cup butter, melted
1 egg yolk
1 tablespoon water

1. Combine the graham crackers, sugar, and salt in a medium bowl with a fork until mixed completely. Add the melted butter and continue to mix completely.

2. Pour into a lightly greased 9-inch pie dish and firmly press the mixture into the bottom and sides, using a 1/4-cup measuring cup or tablespoon to form the crust.

3. Whisk together egg yolk and water. Brush crust gently with egg yolk and water mixture until lightly covered.

4. Bake at 350°F for 8 minutes.

My aunt Margie made many pies with this special graham cracker crust, and my twin sister and I loved to help her crush the crackers!

# Sweetie-licious Coconut Graham Cracker Crust

1/2 cup crushed graham crackers
1/2 cup coconut
1/4 cup sugar
Dash of salt
6 tablespoons butter, melted

1. Combine the graham crackers, coconut, sugar, and salt in a medium bowl with a fork until mixed completely. Add the melted butter and continue to mix completely.

2. Pour into a lightly greased 9-inch pie dish and firmly press the mixture into the bottom and sides, using a 1/4-cup measuring cup or tablespoon to form the crust.

3. Bake at 350°F for 10 minutes.

# Sweetie-licious Chocolate Graham Cracker Crust

1 1/2 cups crushed chocolate graham crackers
3 tablespoons sugar
1/8 teaspoon salt
1/3 cup butter, melted
1 egg yolk
1 tablespoon water

1. Combine the graham crackers, sugar, and salt in a medium bowl with a fork until mixed completely. Add the melted butter and continue to mix completely.

2. Pour into a lightly greased 9-inch pie dish and firmly press the mixture into the bottom and sides, using a 1/4-cup measuring cup or tablespoon to form the crust.

3. Whisk together egg yolk and water. Brush crust gently with egg yolk and water mixture until lightly covered.

4. Bake at 350°F for 8 minutes.

Always make more than one piecrust and keep them in the freezer so you can "whip up" a homemade pie in no time at all!

# Sweetie-licious Crumb Topping

2/3 cup flour
1/4 cup sugar
1/8 teaspoon salt
3 tablespoons butter, softened

Mix all of the ingredients together in a stand mixer using the paddle attachment until the butter is combined and the texture is fine.

You can change up crumb toppings by adding just a few nuts or 1/4 cup oatmeal or brown sugar in place of sugar—be creative!

# Sweetie-licious Praline Pecans

1 cup pecans, chopped
2 tablespoons butter
2 tablespoons brown sugar

1. In a nonstick skillet, combine the pecans, butter, and brown sugar. Cook on low heat until you smell the pecans roasting.

2. Remove from the heat, cool on aluminum foil, and set aside.

Not all recipes require a cup of pecans. If you have extra, note that these freeze beautifully, ready to be used in pancakes, muffins, or quick breads, over ice cream, and so on.

# Homemade Caramel Sauce

14 ounces sweetened condensed milk
1 cup light corn syrup
1 cup sugar
1/2 cup brown sugar
1/4 cup butter
1 tablespoon vanilla extract

1. In a heavy 3-quart saucepan, combine the condensed milk, corn syrup, sugar, brown sugar, and butter.

2. Cook over medium heat, stirring constantly, covering all parts of the bottom of the pan with a wire whisk to prevent scorching. Stir until the mixture comes to a boil.

3. Reduce the heat to low and continue stirring until the caramel reaches 244°F on a candy thermometer, or a firm ball stage.

4. Remove from the heat and add the vanilla. Let the sauce cool and set aside.

# Sweetie-licious Whipped Cream

1 pint heavy whipping cream
1/4 cup confectioners' sugar
1/2 teaspoon vanilla extract

In a medium bowl, mix all of the ingredients using a hand mixer or stand mixer (stand mixer preferred) until thick and creamy.

# Rolling Love

I love a good rolling pin, especially the old ones that have seen many a piecrust in their day. I have had a dear collection of rolling pins throughout my baking career, most of which are now scattered around my pie shop. Through the years I would pick them up at secondhand stores for a few dollars, mainly because I couldn't bear to see them forgotten. I love thinking of their former owners. I believe these rolling pins all to be expert pie makers, generally because of the patina of the wood and the worn colors on the handles. Clearly, given their condition, they either tried for years to make a good pie or simply made good pie for years. (I am sure it is the latter.) I am also convinced that these pins were the magic wands of our foremother pie bakers, the ones who knew the truth in a flaky piecrust and the honesty in a velvet pie filling. Much the way a musician needs to be "as one" with his instrument, a pie baker needs to be "as one" with her pin.

My favorite pin is a sentimental choice, as it was my lovely mother's. She received it for a wedding gift some fifty-eight years ago. She used it for years, pumping out hundreds of delicious and unforgettable pies. Her rolling pin certainly left more than a passing impression on me. Whenever I saw the pin on the kitchen counter as I was growing up, I knew it was time to rejoice, for a pie was to be enjoyed in my near future. When I married twenty-eight years ago, my mother handed down her beloved rolling pin to me. I happily honed my pie-baking skills with my dear rolling pin when I was a new wife, as my children grew, and then at my dreamy pie shop.

I loved rolling pie dough with my heirloom rolling pin. Unfortunately, after fifty-eight years and thousands and thousands of piecrusts, its bearings have finally worn out. My dear pin has clearly earned its time to rest and its special place of honor at home. It sits humbly on my kitchen shelf, admired and respected for its wondrous body of work and its tireless contribution of . . . changing the world one pie at a time!

*Eat pie, love life.*

## Chapter 1

# CHARACTER

*"Manners — the final and perfect flower of noble character."*

—William Winter

I think building a strong character is one of the most challenging virtues of all. Most of us have had some type of instruction as to what is right and wrong, but keeping those teachings in line with what we say and do can be daunting at times. I find that those with strong character intend to see integrity and goodwill persevere, no matter the circumstances. Although people's will may weaken through life, those with strong character always find the strength to carry on. There is always room to polish up our own character with making good decisions, thinking of others first, believing in our neighbors, and being a fair leader, to name a few. For to better our own character is essential not only for ourselves, but for all those we influence every day.

We must always find enough courage to do the right thing, and to make a flaky piecrust!

# Tom's Cheery Cherry Cherry Berry Pie

## Eat pie, inspire others.

My brother-in-law Tom was one of those whom you instinctively loved and respected. Everyone was drawn in by his mile-wide smile, which he used sincerely and often. After you got to know Tom, you respected him for his passions, his work ethic, his commitments, his loyalty, his strength, and his love for all living things. As our brother, neighbor, and friend, his good deeds to our family are too numerous to mention, but a particular passion of his was especially dear to me—his love for all things pie! Every week or so we'd have the family over for "movie night," for which Tom's beloved wife, also named Linda, and I do potluck and the rest of the family indulges in a feast, with of course plenty of pie for dessert. The next morning, without fail, Tom would track me down to give me a quick message, as Hundt men, by nature, are men of few words. His words were simple, yet the happiness they gave me was powerful: "Linda, the cherry pie you made last night was absolutely outstanding." I could see his smile, his conviction, and his kindness over the phone line. I would thank him profusely and go on with my day with much more confidence, zeal, and inspiration because of him. Although he is no longer with us, Tom Hundt understood the most significant creeds to live by, and he continues to inspire others to be outstanding in everything they do.

**Recommended: Flaky Classic Piecrust, frozen (page 1), Sweetie-licious Crumb Topping (page 6)**

**Filling**
6 cups Montmorency tart cherries, frozen
1/4 cup dried Michigan cherries
1 cup sugar
1/4 cup cornstarch
1/2 teaspoon almond extract
1 teaspoon lemon juice, fresh squeezed
1/2 teaspoon orange zest
2 1/2 cups fresh or frozen blueberries

1. Preheat the oven to 375°F.

2. In a medium saucepan, combine the frozen cherries, dried cherries, sugar, and cornstarch. Stir constantly on medium-high heat until boiling.

3. Boil for 1 minute, stirring constantly, until thickened.

4. Remove from the heat and add the almond extract, lemon juice, and orange zest.

5. Pour the frozen blueberries on the bottom of a frozen piecrust. Top with the cooked fruit filling, and cover completely with Crumb Topping.

6. Bake for an hour or more or until the pie filling bubbles over.

7. Cool on a rack and keep at room temperature.

Need a pie to win a guy? Master this recipe. NPC Best in Show, Food Network Pie Challenge winner—this pie is the most popular at our shop, and all men love it!

# Grandma Ferrell's Charismatic Fresh Strawberry & Cream Pie

## Eat pie, be charming.

My mother grew up in rural West Virginia, and every year their little town hosted a very popular Strawberry Festival. This festival attracted people from around the state—perfect for my grandmother Ferrell, who owned an old boardinghouse with a small but adorable restaurant on the back porch. In the early summer, when strawberries were in season and the festival was in full swing, Grandma's house was bustling with guests. People loved to stay there because not only was she a warm and loving hostess, but she happened to make the best strawberry cream pie in the state. They lined up the street for her tender crust, creamy filling, and sweet berry slice of heaven. Grandma's beautiful personality and perfect pie made people come again and again to enjoy her charm and baking talents.

Recommended: Flaky Classic Piecrust, frozen (page 1)

1. Preheat the oven to 375°F.

2. Line a frozen piecrust with one layer of aluminum foil and fill with one layer of uncooked pasta.

3. Bake in the oven until the bottom of the crust is light brown, approximately 25 minutes.

4. Carefully lift the pasta-filled foil from the crust. Let the crust cool.

5. Continue with the directions for the filling on page 21.

**Filling**
2 1/2 cups milk
3 egg yolks
1 cup sugar
Dash of salt
1/4 cup cornstarch
1 tablespoon butter
1 tablespoon vanilla extract
1/4 teaspoon almond extract

> "The great hope of society is individual character."
> —William Ellery Channing

1. Mix the milk, egg yolks, sugar, salt, and cornstarch in a medium pan.
2. Cook on medium heat, stirring constantly until thick.
3. Add the butter, vanilla, and almond extract.
4. Pour the filling into the piecrust and refrigerate for at least 3 hours.

**Fresh Strawberry Glaze**
1 1/2 cups fresh strawberries, sliced and mashed
3/4 cup sugar
1/2 cup water
1/4 cup cornstarch
1/8 teaspoon orange zest
4 cups fresh strawberries, sliced

1. Mix the mashed strawberries, sugar, water, cornstarch, and orange zest in a medium pan on low to medium heat until thickened. Chill until cold.
2. In a large bowl, add the 4 cups fresh strawberry slices to the strawberry glaze, stirring until they are completely coated.
3. Top the pie with the strawberry glaze.
4. Keep refrigerated. Best eaten on the first day.

Like any pie that calls for fresh fruit, this pie is so much better with in-season fruit when the natural sweetness and flavor are at their peak! Fresh fruit also has the right amount of juices to make a delicious filling.

# My Hometown

Since I was a little girl, I have always been so proud of my home state, Michigan. I love the way Michiganders experience the seasons, each one vibrant and defined by its color, temperature, pastimes—and the food it brings to the table! Whether you are picking fruits or vegetables from a tree, bush, or garden, Michigan's seasonal bounty is plentiful. Our recreation even pairs with the seasons: Water and snow sports are beloved Michigan activities.

Our state is beautiful, filled with glorious deciduous and pine trees, acres of open farm fields, and miles and miles of sandy beaches. Michigan's little towns are slow-paced and peaceful, while our big cities are cultural and vivacious. And Michiganders are typical midwestern folks—hardworking, humble, of great character, with sweet and easy dispositions.

My hometown, DeWitt, is as cute as you can imagine. It is, indeed, a place where people know you by name and where little parades, farm markets, and festivals line our streets. Everyone turns out for Friday-night football games, and the tiny barbershop is standing room only on Saturday mornings.

My sweet hometown folks have always been supportive of my little pie shop, and me! They came and bought pies, cookies, and lunch. They told their friends, who bought more pies. The friends brought in their relatives, and they bought muffins and even more pies. And so on, and so on. I can never thank DeWitt enough for helping make Sweetie-licious the success that it is and—more important—for believing in me.

I wish everyone the privilege of living in a place of camaraderie like DeWitt, Michigan. It's a town I am proud to be from, and one I hope I make proud!

*Eat pie, love life.*

# Abe Lincoln's Selfless Cherry Apple Pie

## Eat pie, be a selfless dreamer.

Abraham Lincoln and I share a birthday. I have felt honored all my life that such a beloved man had anything in common with oh, so simple me. I am always boasting about my Abe, as if he were a dear grandfather. He possessed two virtues that I believe are paramount: the ability to dream and to be selfless. People who live their lives selflessly understand their purpose. Abraham understood that standing up for what is good and just, loving all living beings equally, and living your life doing good for others are the secrets to life. He started off no different from you and me, neither a king nor God. He was merely an ordinary midwestern man who did extraordinary things because he realized his cause was bigger than himself and dreamed that he could make the world better—and of course he did. God bless Abe!

**Recommended: Flaky Classic Piecrust, frozen (page 1), Sweetie-licious Crumb Topping (page 6)**

**Apple Filling**
3 cups peeled, small-diced Michigan
    Cortland or Ida Red apples
1/2 cup sugar
2 teaspoons flour
2 tablespoons butter, melted
1 teaspoon cinnamon
1/2 teaspoon lemon juice
1/8 teaspoon salt

**Cherry Filling**
4 cups frozen unsweetened pitted
    Michigan tart red cherries
3/4 cup sugar
3 tablespoons cornstarch
1/2 teaspoon lemon juice

1. Preheat the oven to 375°F.

2. Mix the apples, sugar, flour, butter, cinnamon, lemon juice, and salt in a large bowl until well blended. Set aside.

3. Combine the cherries, sugar, cornstarch, and lemon juice in a medium pan. Cook on medium heat, stirring constantly until thickened.

4. Put the apple mixture in the bottom of a frozen pie shell. Pour the cherry filling over the apple mixture almost to the top of the crust.

5. Cover with Crumb Topping, covering all of the pie filling. Bake for an hour or more, or until the pie filling bubbles over.

6. Cool on a rack and keep at room temperature.

 Abraham Lincoln loved pies, especially apple!

# Theda's Unique Peanut Butter Coconut Banana Cream Pie

Eat pie, be the real you.

My aunt Theda was definitely one of a kind—eccentric, fun, and someone who did everything her own way. She was known for her love of church, bugs, garage sales, and, especially, food! While growing up, we always made a stop at her quaint little house in West Virginia on our way to my grandparents' farm. One time I watched as she packed us sandwiches in an unconventional manner that I loved, piling each slice of bread with peanut butter and various other condiments; some had sweet and dill pickles, others bananas and coconut, some were topped with raisins and carrots, and some were even topped with bacon and onion. Though shocked, my family enjoyed the creative sandwiches, but I absolutely loved them all, especially the banana coconut peanut butter one, the inspiration for this pie.

**Recommended: Sweetie-licious Coconut Graham Cracker Crust (page 3)**

**Filling**
3 cups milk
3 egg yolks
1/2 cup brown sugar
1/2 cup sugar
Dash of salt
1/4 cup plus 1 tablespoon cornstarch
1 teaspoon vanilla extract
1/3 cup peanut butter

1/2 cup toasted coconut
2 bananas

**Garnish—Optional**
Sweetie-licious Whipped Cream (see
  recipe on page 8)
Toasted coconut
Peanut butter cookies, crumbled

1. Combine milk, egg yolks, sugars, salt, and cornstarch.

2. Cook over medium heat until boiling. Boil for 1 minute, stirring constantly.

3. Add the vanilla, peanut butter, and 1/2 cup toasted coconut.

4. Whisk until completely blended.

5. Pour half of the filling into the crust. Slice the bananas and layer the slices onto the filling.

6. Pour the remaining filling on top.

7. Cover with plastic wrap and refrigerate for at least 3 hours.

8. Decorate with Whipped Cream, toasted coconut, and crumbled peanut butter cookies.

# Daddy's Apple Mince Pie

Eat pie, respect your elders.

My daddy grew up on a farm in Michigan during the Great Depression. Although he was an only child, his extended family was large and lived on farms close by. Sunday and holiday dinners were much anticipated and memorable, especially Thanksgiving and Christmas when grandparents, aunts, uncles, and cousins flooded my great-grandfather's large farmhouse for a lovely, festive dinner. There were plenty of traditional midwestern foods that the family contributed straight from the fruit cellar: canned vegetables, cranberry relish and pickles, as well as various potato dishes, stuffing, turkey, ham, and many homemade pies!

My father's family is known for storytelling, and my daddy loved hearing the tales that his uncles and other relatives would tell of the good old days. Some of their conversations were funny, some thoughtful, some historical, but all of them were entertaining. Back then children were taught to respect their elders by being quiet and listening without speaking up. He remembered that he and his cousins filled his older relatives' plates with pie all afternoon while listening to their anecdotes. These family stories, filled with love and respect, were passed on to all who knew him.

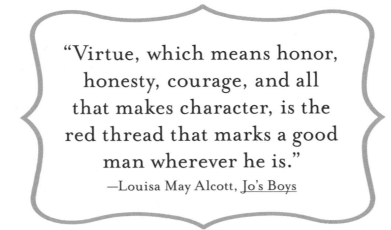

"Virtue, which means honor, honesty, courage, and all that makes character, is the red thread that marks a good man wherever he is."
—Louisa May Alcott, Jo's Boys

**Recommended: Flaky Classic Piecrust, frozen (page 1), Sweetie-licious Crumb Topping (page 6)**

**Filling**

5 cups peeled, cored, and sliced Ida Red or Granny Smith apples

1 1/2 cups dark or golden raisins

1 cup pecans, chopped

1 cup brown sugar

3/4 teaspoon salt

1/2 cup apple cider

1/4 cup brandy

1/4 cup unsalted butter

Grated zest of 1/2 orange

Grated zest of 1/2 lemon

2 teaspoons balsamic vinegar

1 tablespoon flour

1 1/2 teaspoons cinnamon

1 teaspoon nutmeg, freshly grated or ground

1/4 teaspoon cloves

1. Preheat the oven to 350°F.

2. In a large saucepan, mix all of the ingredients and cook on medium heat until the apples are tender, approximately 12 minutes. Stir frequently.

3. Pour the filling into the frozen pie shell. Sprinkle with Crumb Topping until all of the pie filling is covered.

4. Bake for 45 minutes or until the pie filling bubbles over.

You can exchange walnuts for pecans in this old-fashioned pie, and it will be equally delicious!

# Jordyn's True Champion Blueberry Raspberry Cherry Pie

Eat pie, be a true champion in all that you do.

All of us have the ability to be some kind of champion. Some of us will be champions at county fairs, singing competitions, spelling bees, art competitions, or even pie-baking contests. Some will be champions for admirable charities and causes, or for how we raise our children, or in later life for how we care for our parents. Some will be champion athletes—from Little League to high school state championships to the Olympics. We all know that no one can be a champion without passion, perseverance, and innate talent. However, what sets a true champion apart is grace: the ability to lose with grace and honor and win with humble pride and joy. Our hometown sweetheart, Olympic gold medal gymnast Jordyn Wieber, is such a true champion. Let us all emulate Jordyn and take home the gold in our everyday life, and we will start changing the world one pie at a time!

**Recommended: Flaky Classic Piecrust, frozen (page 1), Sweetie-licious Crumb Topping (page 6)**

**Filling**
5 1/2 cups blueberries, fresh or frozen
3/4 cup sugar
3 tablespoons cornstarch, sifted
1 tablespoon fresh lime juice
1/2 teaspoon fresh orange zest
1 1/2 cups fresh or frozen cherries
1 cup fresh blueberries

1. Preheat the oven to 350°F.

2. Mix the frozen blueberries, sugar, and cornstarch in a large pan on medium heat.

3. Stir constantly until the mixture thickens and boils. Remove from the heat. Add the lime juice and orange zest.

4. Pour the cherries and fresh blueberries into a frozen pie shell. Top with the cooked blueberry filling. Sprinkle with Crumb Topping until all of the pie filling is covered.

5. Bake for 45–60 minutes or until the pie filling bubbles over.

Blueberries have a natural thickener, so most of the time you won't need to use as much thickener as you would with, say, strawberries. I think Michigan has the best blueberries and cherries!

# My Brothers' Creamy Caramel Cashew Pie

## Eat pie, have a forgiving heart.

While I was growing up, I remember my three older brothers, Mark, Paul, and David, constantly eating, as growing boys do. When all five of us kids came home hungry from school, it was definitely every man for himself as we charged into the kitchen. Sandwiches, cereal, and any food without a note on it from Mom telling us not to eat it was fair game. With three hungry boys in the mix, there were sometimes small squabbles.

One day my father, an elementary school principal, was a given a big can of cashews from a parent or teacher. When he brought it home, we all went crazy with excitement, for we were a family that loved nuts but seldom got cashews because they were so expensive. My father was particularly fond of nuts and was very excited about the gift as well. The next day my young brothers simply could not resist the cashews for their after-school snack. Intending to eat just a few, they instead ate every single cashew from the can while riveted by *Star Trek* reruns. They were instantly full of regret for their nut-eating binge, and felt horrible that Daddy didn't get any of his beloved cashews. My father was clearly disappointed, but saw the remorseful look in my brothers' eyes, smiled a forgiving smile, and claimed he would have done the same thing.

As it was, the cashew incident inspired a new Christmas tradition for our family. Every year from then on, each of my brothers would give my father a can of nuts under the tree, and my daddy would add a Planters nut candy bar in each of our Christmas stockings.

**Recommended: Sweetie-licious Cream Cheese Crust, frozen (page 2)**

**Filling**
1 cup butter, melted
1 cup brown sugar
2 tablespoons flour
2 tablespoons Buttershots liqueur
2 teaspoons vanilla extract
3 eggs, room temperature
1 cup toffee bits
2 cups cashews, chopped
3/4 cup whipping cream

**Garnish—Optional**
Homemade Caramel Sauce (see recipe on page 7)
Toffee bits

1. Preheat the oven to 375°F.

2. Mix all of the ingredients together and pour into a frozen pie shell.

3. Bake for 40–50 minutes or until the pie is set in the middle.

4. Drizzle with Caramel Sauce and toffee bits, if desired.

This pie is sooo delicious warmed up and served with really good vanilla bean ice cream!

Chapter 2

# FAITH

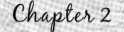

*"The most real things in the world
are those that neither children
nor grown-ups can see."*

—Francis P. Church

For me the very best thing about growing older has been recognizing the importance of my faith and the beautiful power
that resonates from my soul. It has ener-
gized me like no yoga class ever could.
Having faith in all people, believing in
them and yourself, is truly another secret
to life. Faith affirms our purpose and also
reminds us that we are never alone. Its
presence in our hearts allows us to see beyond melancholy
days, through to glorious tomorrows. Faith lets us appreciate
our past, accept our present, and anticipate our future.

Our lives should be filled with faith: in God, ourselves, our
neighbors, and our ability to make a lovely piecrust!

# Johnny's Creamy Coconut Cream Pie

Eat pie, never stop trying.

One of my most memorable dates with my then-future husband was a picnic in the park. I wanted to display my cooking talents to my new beau, so I planned to make everything myself: fried chicken, coleslaw, baked beans, and coconut cream pie. I had helped my mom in the kitchen my whole life, so none of this was daunting for me—except the elusive piecrust.

I spent an hour trying to roll out the pie dough, but had failed miserably each and every time. I was ready to quit when my mother walked into the kitchen after a long day at work. She saw my despair and patiently taught me the art of pie baking.

The pie was delicious, the picnic a success, and we were engaged a few short years later. To this day, my husband claims he was ready to ask me to marry him at our first picnic, because I made such a delicious pie. Oh, the power of pie.

**Recommended: Sweetie-licious Coconut Graham Cracker Crust (page 3)**

**Filling**
1 1/3 cups from a 15-ounce can cream of coconut (the kind used as an alcoholic drink mixer)
2 cups whole milk
4 egg yolks
1/4 cup cornstarch
Dash of salt
1 tablespoon butter
1 cup sweetened shredded coconut
1/2 teaspoon vanilla extract
1/4 teaspoon almond extract

1. Mix the cream of coconut, milk, egg yolks, cornstarch, and salt in a medium pan.

2. Cook on medium heat, stirring constantly until thick.

3. Remove from the heat and add the butter, coconut, and vanilla and almond extracts.

4. Pour the filling into a piecrust and refrigerate for at least 3 hours.

Always use real butter, not margarine, in these recipes, as well as whatever milk or cream is called for. Substituting skim milk can affect the pie's texture, flavor, and overall success.

# The Farmette's Blueberry Basil Cream Pie

## Eat pie, believe in yourself.

I remember how excited I was when we bought our old farmhouse, which came complete with barns, fruit trees, and berry bushes. It was a dream come true. I could hardly wait to cook and bake new creations for my lovely family with our own produce! As we expanded our gardens, my husband and I planted lots of herbs with our vegetables, as I loved the taste of fresh herbs in my cooking. As the summers passed and I became more confident and creative with my pies and jams, I blended the fragrant essence of the herbs and citrus zest with the sweet, homegrown fruits to make amazing taste sensations. Soon I started selling my work at farm markets and local high-end restaurants, with my blueberry, basil, and lime jam being a customer and chef favorite and the inspiration for this pie. There have been skeptics about this combination of flavors—until they try it, and then they become believers too!

**Recommended: Flaky Classic Piecrust, frozen (page 1)**

1. Preheat the oven to 375°F.
2. Line a frozen piecrust with one layer of aluminum foil and fill with one layer of uncooked pasta.
3. Bake in the oven until the bottom of the crust is light brown, approximately 25 minutes.
4. Carefully lift the foil from the crust. Let the crust cool.
5. Continue with the filling directions on next page.

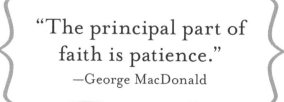

"The principal part of faith is patience."
—George MacDonald

**Filling**
2¹/₂ cups whole milk
3 egg yolks
1 cup sugar
¹/₄ cup cornstarch
Dash of salt
1 tablespoon butter
1 tablespoon vanilla extract

1. Mix the milk, egg yolks, sugar, cornstarch, and salt in a medium pan.

2. Cook on medium heat, stirring constantly until thick.

3. Add the butter and vanilla.

4. Pour the filling into the piecrust.

5. Refrigerate for at least 3 hours.

**Fresh Blueberry Glaze**

1¹/₂ cups fresh blueberries, mashed
1 cup sugar
³/₄ cup water
¹/₄ cup cornstarch, sifted
6 large fresh basil leaves, preferably in
    cheesecloth herb bag

1 teaspoon fresh lime juice
¹/₄ teaspoon fresh orange zest
4 cups fresh blueberries

**Garnish—Optional**
Fresh basil leaves

1. Mix the mashed blueberries, sugar, water, and cornstarch in a large pan on medium heat.

2. Stir constantly until thick and boiling.

3. Add the basil leaves in a cheesecloth bag or tied together. Carefully stir for 1 minute, then remove from the heat.

4. Remove the basil leaves. Add the lime juice and orange zest.

5. Refrigerate for 3 hours.

6. In a large bowl, mix the glaze with 4 cups fresh blueberries. Pour over the pie filling.

7. Garnish with fresh basil leaves. Keep refrigerated. Best eaten on the first day.

Always use the best ingredients you can buy. Quality ingredients guarantee a quality pie!

# Home

I am not sure there is a more revered word than *home*. For me, no matter how tiring, frustrating, or melancholy my day might be, when I drive into my old farmhouse's driveway, my heart is filled with a soft and joyful peace.

Home is where our hearts stand still with tranquility. Just the thought of home takes us back to a world of love and serenity—where all is right with the world.

We all long for this ideal home. It's where comfort and love live forever. It's a place of rock-solid reassurance and acceptance. It's where our parents, grandparents, brothers, sisters, children, and friends are waiting for us with open arms and smiling faces. Home is where all of us belong.

And nothing, nothing takes you home like a piece of homemade pie!

*Eat pie, love life.*

# Katherine's Roasted Pepper Feta Company Quiche

## Eat pie, be joyfully faithful!

One of my favorite women of all time was my cousin Katherine from West Virginia. I so admired her jubilant and faithful spirit; she simply spilled joy in all that she did, as she smiled her way through life. When she was excited about something, which she often was, she would say while grinning, "Well, butter my biscuit!" I loved that!

I loved her way of faith, as she never wore it on her sleeve, but would make subtle comments and clever quips about God, as if the two of them were best friends. When someone was sad or downtrodden about something, she would say to them, "Honey, all you need is faith as itty-bitty as a mustard seed, and nothing is impossible."

Katherine was also an amazing cook, and I was crazy for everything she made in her tiny kitchen. When our family came down to visit, she would welcome us with a huge West Virginia–style breakfast: biscuits, apple butter and honey, sausage gravy, ham, fried apples and corn, sliced cantaloupe, and her big, fluffy company quiche pies. Everything about Katherine was lovable, and she knew how to live her life with a happy faith that I try to emulate every day.

**Recommended: Sweetie-licious Cream Cheese Crust, frozen (page 2)**

**Filling**
7 eggs
1 1/4 cups half-and-half
1/2 teaspoon garlic salt
2 teaspoons Italian seasoning
1/4 teaspoon pepper, or to taste
1 1/2 cups canned roasted red peppers, well drained and set on paper towels
1/2 cup crumbled feta cheese
4 large basil leaves, chopped fine

1. Preheat the oven to 375°F.

2. In a medium bowl, whisk the eggs, half-and-half, garlic salt, Italian seasoning, and pepper until well mixed.

3. On the bottom of the frozen piecrust, layer the roasted red peppers, feta, and basil leaves.

4. Carefully pour the egg mixture over the peppers, feta, and basil.

5. Bake for 45–60 minutes or until the middle is set. Best served warm.

This quiche is a favorite at the shop!

# The Little Miracle Fresh Rhubarb Custard Pie

Eat pie, believe in little miracles.

A few years back I went into the shop one early-May morning to start my baking. One of the orders in the book was for a rhubarb custard pie. Sometimes the high school counter girls accidentally took orders for pies that were out of season, such as this one. As it was a little too early in the year to be getting deliveries of fresh rhubarb, I called up my husband to ask him if we had any ready in our own little patch at home. John said that there were a few stalks and brought them over.

As I was cutting up the rhubarb, I realized I'd have enough for two pies, instead of just one, and looked forward to taking the bonus one home, as it was our family's favorite. While the pies were baking, two older women came into the shop looking quite distressed, as they were lost trying to find their way to Saginaw, an hour away. I gave them directions and invited them to stay and have some quiche and pleasant conversation. They agreed to stay and eat. They enjoyed delicious quiche and warm muffins while I continued to bake and wait on customers. Each time I checked on them they seemed calmer and happier. The elder of the two said that the shop made her feel so contented, she was happy she and her daughter had gotten lost and found our cute little pie shop!

She then introduced herself as Mary and went on to explain that she lived in Florida and hadn't been back to Michigan in forty years. She had come to spend some last days with her dying brother. Mary told me, with a slight smile, that while sitting in the shop, she got lost in the old music and the wonderful aroma of pies, and suddenly was reminded of her dying brother's favorite pie. She thought it would be a wonderful gift to give her brother in hospice care, if I happened to have it: a rhubarb custard pie.

I couldn't believe my ears! I could not believe that she wanted *the* pie that I only had because of an ordering mistake, that there just happened to be enough rhubarb to make not just one accidental pie, but two, and that this all happened that day, that morning, at the exact time the pie was miraculously coming out of the oven.

Tears streamed down my face when I told her, yes, we did happen to have one. I explained the whole story. I hugged her with pot holders in my hands and held this elderly lady as we both cried tears of melancholy joy and understanding in the miracle of pie.

> "In the faces of men and women, I see God."
> —Walt Whitman

**Recommended: Flaky Classic Piecrust, frozen (page 1), Sweetie-licious Crumb Topping (page 6)**

**Rhubarb Filling**
5 cups sliced fresh rhubarb
1¹/₂ cups sugar
¹/₄ cup tapioca (minute variety)
¹/₂ teaspoon orange zest

**Custard Filling**
1¹/₄ cups half-and-half
2 eggs
¹/₄ sugar
¹/₄ teaspoon vanilla extract
¹/₈ teaspoon almond extract

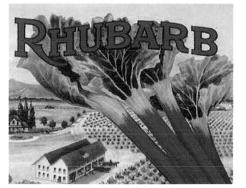

1. Preheat the oven to 375°F.

2. In a large mixing bowl, combine the rhubarb, sugar, tapioca, and zest. Stir until well mixed.

3. Let stand for 20–25 minutes or until the tapioca is softened to the touch, occasionally stirring the fruit.

4. Mix all of the ingredients for the custard filling with a whisk until well combined.

5. Pour the rhubarb filling into a frozen piecrust. Pour the custard filling over the rhubarb. Cover all of pie filling with Crumb Topping, being especially generous around the edges.

6. Bake for 45–60 minutes or until the filling bubbles over. Best eaten on first day.

This is a family favorite—we make this pie for all summer birthdays and holidays!

I have found that different thickeners work better in different pies. Flour works well with apples, cornstarch with frozen fruits, and tapioca with fresh fruits.

> "Now faith is being sure of what we hope
> for and certain of what we do not see."
> —The Book of Hebrews

# Summer Picnics

I am convinced that our Michigan summers are the best summers anywhere. They are generally not too humid, nor too cold; they offer just the right amount of sunshine to make picnics, days at the beach, and backyard barbecues perfect pastimes.

My childhood family picnics are some of my most treasured summer memories. It seems like more people went on picnics back then. There were church picnics, company picnics, end-of-school picnics, reunion picnics, and family picnics. I remember many a weekend with my mother packing a lovely spread on Saturday night; the next day we would go on a Sunday drive to an area park to enjoy our family dinner. She usually had fried chicken, potato salad, carrot and celery sticks, deviled eggs, cut melon, cold pork and beans out of a can (not a favorite), and a yummy dessert.

We picnicked on family vacations, of course, and when it rained we would have our picnics inside the old woody station wagon. This was always a little chaotic with eight people: my parents, six kids (we always took our best friend, Sheila), a dog, and lots of luggage crammed in the hot, non-air-conditioned family vehicle. My mother had little individual baskets with our name written on a napkin tucked inside. She packed each one identically, so there were no arguments, from her front-seat makeshift kitchen. I remember each of us wanting to get our lunch basket first, for it took some time to get through eight lunches, and certainly the last one fed could easily get shortchanged an apple slice or potato chip! While these lunches were a little plain, they were clearly the highlight of the long, hot car rides.

Why not take your loved ones to a nearby park or beach with a basket full of yummy food? To make your picnic extra special, of course, bring along a pie!

*Eat pie, love life.*

# Mr. Spagnuolo's Sweet Onion Cheese Pie

Eat pie, believe in others.

Mr. Spag, as he was fondly called, was my English teacher all through high school. He introduced me to the written word, and to how words can change people and, ultimately, the way we choose to live. He taught me to examine, imagine, create, articulate, work hard, be passionate, believe, and dream. He inspired me, and he believed in me.

Truly, many people affect how we create our own lives, and make no mistake: We do create our own lives. However, sometimes certain people carve their initials into our souls and enable us to see our potential, our gifts, and our own utopia. Mr. Spag did this for me. He told me I was smart and that if I worked hard I could accomplish much. He told me I had gifts. He told me to dream. He believed in me. I was astounded that a man of his merit thought all of this of me, little Linda McComb. In retrospect, I see that I did exactly what he taught me to: I dreamed, I created, I used my passion and gifts, and I worked hard, very hard, to create the life I want and the world I want to live in, to share with my family and friends and now my customers.

If I had not been blessed to have him as my teacher all those years ago, I would not be everything I am today, nor everything I will be tomorrow.

**Recommended: Flaky Classic Piecrust, frozen (page 1)**

**Filling**
5 cups sliced sweet Vidalia onions
2 teaspoons brown sugar
1 tablespoon white wine
3 tablespoons butter
1 tablespoon finely cut fresh tarragon
1 teaspoon garlic salt
1/8 teaspoon pepper
1 1/2 cups heavy cream
1/2 cup milk
2 eggs
1 tablespoon flour
1 1/2 cups grated gruyère or swiss cheese

1. Preheat the oven to 350°F.

2. Cook the onions, brown sugar, wine, butter, and tarragon in a very large pot or frying pan on low to medium heat, stirring frequently until the onions are tender and caramelized.

3. In a medium-size bowl, whisk the garlic salt, pepper, cream, milk, and eggs until well mixed.

4. In a new medium bowl, mix the flour and cheese together.

5. On the bottom of a frozen piecrust, layer the caramelized onions and cheese, then carefully pour the cream-and-egg mixture over the shell, patting down the cheese and onions so that the cream mixture is completely covering them.

6. Bake for 45–60 minutes or until the middle is set.

7. Best served warm with salad and/or fresh fruit. This is very rich, so it goes a long way—perfect for holiday brunches!

This pie was inspired by an onion pie that is famous in Strasbourg, France, a city we learned about in Mr. Spag's class.

# Mothers' Easy Peach Crisp Pie

Eat pie, believe in yourself.

Years ago, while tucking my sweet girls into bed, they shared that one of their favorite words was *Mommy*. I have never felt more accomplished.

I remember sitting on my own mother's lap as a child, pushing her face toward mine so I could stare at her loving smile as she read to me. That memory still warms my heart like no other.

Mothers offer our hearts an unconditional love and sanctuary that can never be duplicated. I often think of the centuries of soldiers dying on battlefields, calling out for their dear mothers for a measure of peace and love in their last breaths. For at the end of the day, as beaten and melancholy as we may be, our hearts are lightened knowing that at the very least, our mothers still love and believe in us.

Yes, mothers are human beings, and flawed like all people. But I do believe it is a good thing to put mothers on a well-deserved pedestal for their steadfast, deep devotion to their children. My mother made pie, as so many mothers before us have done, to warm our souls, comfort our bodies, and feel her love!

**Recommended: Sweetie-licious Crumb Topping (page 6)**

**Filling**
1 (29-ounce) can sliced peaches, well
    drained
1/2 cup brown sugar
3 tablespoons flour
Dash of salt

1/2 teaspoon cinnamon
1/4 teaspoon almond extract
1/4 teaspoon vanilla extract
1/4 cup heavy cream

"All that I am, or hope to be,
I owe to my angel mother."
—Abraham Lincoln

1. Preheat the oven to 375°F.

2. In a medium bowl, combine all of the ingredients until well mixed.

3. Butter a 9-inch pie pan or tart pan.

4. Pour the peach filling into the pan.

5. Spread the Crumb Topping mixture on top of the peach filling until all of the filling is covered.

6. Place on a foiled cookie sheet and bake for 30 minutes or until the filling bubbles over.

Need a pie in a hurry? This crustless pie recipe is so easy, making it perfect for potlucks, Sunday dinners, and game days!

# Chapter 3

# GRATITUDE

*"The world is so full of a number of things, I'm sure we should all be as happy as Kings."*

*—Robert Louis Stevenson*

Oh, the power of gratitude. Sincere appreciation helps make our lives truly meaningful.

I encourage all of us to verbally express our loving and sincere gratitude to everyone and everything that shelters us, aids us, feeds us, encourages us, and loves us. As we soak up others' generosity, we can stimulate and express our own. In this way we complete the circle of giving and receiving, a circle that spiritually enriches everyone within it. To be grateful for our heart, in its brokenness, its fullness, and its beautiful beat, is the beginning of humble wisdom.

So let's always be thankful for all of life's blessings, and most especially a delicious, homemade pie!

# Mommy's Pineapple Pecan Cheesecake Pie

## Eat pie, feel blessed.

When I think of my mother, I think of her in the kitchen. She loved to cook and bake and deemed these her hobbies. All I know for sure is something magical happened in that tiny, turquoise kitchen, and our family's breakfasts, lunches, and dinners were the miraculous proof. I loved her chicken and dumplings and lasagna, but mostly I loved her pies, especially her pineapple cheesecake pie. Mom traditionally made pies for church potlucks, family reunions, and holiday celebrations, and she always, always brought home an empty pie tin. My daddy always told me how blessed I was to have a mother who could make a perfect pie. I am blessed and so are you, because this is her recipe.

**Recommended: Sweetie-licious Cream Cheese Crust, frozen (page 2)**

### Pineapple Layer
1/2 cup brown sugar
Dash of salt
3 tablespoons cornstarch
1 (8-ounce) can crushed pineapple, undrained

### Cheesecake Layer
1 (8-ounce) package cream cheese, softened
1/2 cup sugar
1/2 teaspoon salt
1/2 cup half-and-half
3 eggs
1 teaspoon vanilla extract
1/4 teaspoon almond extract
1/4 cup Sweetie-licious Praline Pecans (see recipe on page 6)

### Garnish—Optional
Sweetie-licious Whipped Cream (see recipe on page 8)
Fresh or dried pineapple

1. Preheat the oven to 375°F.

2. In a medium saucepan, combine the brown sugar, salt, cornstarch, and pineapple. Cook on low to medium heat, stirring constantly, until the mixture becomes clear and thickens.

3. Take the mixture off the heat and let it cool.

4. In a large bowl using a rotary blender or stand mixer, beat the softened cream cheese until creamy. Add the sugar and salt, mixing until well blended. Blend in the half-and-half, eggs (one at a time), and vanilla and almond extracts.

5. Spread the pineapple mixture onto the bottom of a frozen piecrust. Pour the cheesecake mixture over the pineapple. Sprinkle ¼ cup Praline Pecans over the pineapple mixture.

6. Bake for 45 minutes or until the pie is set in the middle and is a light golden color.

7. Refrigerate for at least 3 hours. Garnish with the Whipped Cream and fresh or dried pineapple, if desired.

Always toast or praline your nuts for more depth and richness.

# Grandma Ferrell's Sweetie Pie

## Eat pie, enjoy family traditions.

While I was growing up, my maternal grandmother lived nearly five hundred miles away, so we did not spend the Christmas holidays together. But she always sent our family a Christmas box filled with presents and delicious homemade foods. My brothers and sister and I eagerly anticipated the phone call from the bus station saying that the box had arrived, and we all drove down together in the family station wagon to bring it home. On Christmas morning it was the last box opened, and certainly the sentimental favorite. The gifts were always unpredictable, fun, and silly; the food steadfast, revered, and delicious—especially her beloved Sweetie Pie. The flaky crust, toasted pecans, chocolate, and caramel made for a perfect Christmas Day dessert, particularly because my sweet grandmother made it just for us.

**Recommended: Sweetie-licious Cream Cheese Crust, frozen (page 2)**

**Filling**
$^1$/2 cup unsalted butter, melted
1 cup brown sugar
1 cup evaporated milk
2 tablespoons flour
3 tablespoons Baileys Irish Cream
   or brandy
1 teaspoon vanilla extract
4 eggs, room temperature
1 cup dark chocolate chips
1 cup pecans, toasted and chopped

**Garnish—Optional**
Homemade Caramel Sauce
   (see recipe on page 7)
Chocolate shavings

1. Preheat the oven to 375°F.

2. In a medium mixing bowl, combine all of the pie filling ingredients in the order listed.

3. Pour into a frozen pie shell and bake for 40–45 minutes or until the pie is set. Immediately top with Caramel Sauce and chocolate shavings.

To deepen flavors in baking, use dark brown sugar, or add liqueurs, brandy, or wine.

# Mom's Pretty Pumpkin Pie

## Eat pie, be grateful.

Several years ago a fire burned the home my parents had shared for over forty years. Fortunately, no one was injured, but being out of their home during renovations through the holiday season was difficult. I assured my parents that Christmas would be as special as always and that I would host the dinner. My mother insisted on preparing the holiday ham and pumpkin pies, and my sister and I agreed to make the rest of the trimmings. Since my mother was not familiar with her temporary kitchen, she burned the ham black while our mashed potatoes were lumpy and the cranberries were frozen. Our only salvation through this disastrous dinner was the anticipation of Mom's pumpkin pies. We were not disappointed. The pie had never tasted better; the buttery crust and creamy filling were perfect. They made the meal complete as the whole family realized not only how grateful we were to all be together, alive and healthy, but also how much we appreciate good pie.

**Recommended: Flaky Classic Piecrust, frozen (page 1)**

**Filling**
1¼ cups canned pumpkin
1 cup sugar
1 tablespoon flour
2 teaspoons pumpkin pie spice
¼ teaspoon cloves
¼ teaspoon orange zest

½ teaspoon cinnamon
¼ teaspoon salt
2 eggs, slightly beaten
1 cup half-and-half

**Garnish—Optional**
Freshly grated nutmeg

1. Preheat the oven to 375°F.

2. Combine the pumpkin, sugar, flour, pumpkin pie spice, cloves, orange zest, cinnamon, and salt until well mixed.

3. Add the eggs, mixing well.

4. Mix in the half-and-half until well blended.

5. Pour into a frozen piecrust and bake for 45–50 minutes or until almost set in the middle.

6. Cool. Dust with grated nutmeg.

The orange zest gives this creamy pie delicious depth!

# Grandma Rosella's Fresh Blueberry Pie

## Eat pie, cherish birthdays.

My grandpa was a quiet, melancholy man, unable to find peace after my grandma's death, years before I was born. One summer evening Grandpa and I were talking on his front porch when the subject turned to Grandma's cooking. Suddenly his stoic demeanor changed as he smiled and reminisced about her tender pork roast, bread-and-butter pickles, and delicious blueberry pie. As he shared that my grandma always made a blueberry pie for his birthday, his blue eyes sparkled. He recalled the crust and the sweet berry filling. After hearing his testimony, my mother made sure Grandpa received a birthday blueberry pie for the rest of his years, which made him forever grateful. My grandpa's reverie made me realize at a young age that pie can create unforgettable memories.

**Recommended: Flaky Classic Piecrust, frozen (page 1), Sweetie-licious Crumb Topping (page 6)**

### Filling
5 cups fresh blueberries, partially mashed
3/4 cup sugar
1/4 cup tapioca (minute variety)
1/2 teaspoon orange zest
2 teaspoons fresh lemon juice
2 1/2 cups fresh blueberries

1. Preheat the oven to 375°F.

2. In a medium mixing bowl, combine the mashed blueberries, sugar, tapioca, and orange zest. Stir until well mixed.

3. Let stand for 15 minutes or until the tapioca is softened to the touch.

4. Pour fresh blueberries on the bottom of a frozen piecrust. Top with the blueberry filling.

5. Cover generously with Crumb Topping, covering all of the pie filling and around all the edges.

6. Bake for 50–60 minutes or until the pie filling bubbles over.

One of my all-time favorite pies! Best eaten on the first day.

"I awoke this
morning
with devout
thanksgiving for
my friends."
—Ralph Waldo Emerson

# Laura's Sticky Toffee Pudding Caramel Apple Pie

## Eat pie, appreciate old and new traditions.

My twin sister, Laura, spent several years in British Hong Kong. She had a wonderful experience there with the mixed cultures and foods of myriad people from across the world. Like everyone in our family, my sister especially loved being exposed to diverse foods. Fortunately for the rest of us, she had sticky toffee pudding for dessert one night with some new English friends. She was enamored with the moist caramel cake and creamy sauce and secured the recipe that very evening! She is a wonderful baker and has delighted us with this delicious English dessert ever since. I decided a delicious fusion of this British cake with the all-American caramel apple pie would be wonderful and most appropriate—and it is!

**Recommended: Flaky Classic Piecrust, frozen (page 1), Sweetie-licious Crumb Topping (page 6)**

**Sticky Toffee Pudding Filling**
1/2 cup Sweetie-licious Praline Pecans
   (see recipe on page 6)
1/2 cup butter, softened
1/2 cup brown sugar

2 tablespoons heavy cream
1 tablespoon lemon juice
2 tablespoons water
1 egg, beaten
1/2 cup flour

1. In a medium bowl, combine the Praline Pecans, butter, brown sugar, heavy cream, lemon juice, water, egg, and flour just until blended.

2. Pour onto the bottom of a frozen piecrust.

**Apple Filling**
6 1/2 cups peeled, thinly sliced Michigan
   Cortland or Ida Red apples (5
   medium–large)
1 cup brown sugar
3 tablespoons flour
3 tablespoons butter, melted
2 teaspoons cinnamon

1 teaspoon lemon juice
1/4 teaspoon salt
3/4 cup Homemade Caramel Sauce (see
   recipe on page 7)

**Garnish—Optional**
2 tablespoons Praline Pecans
1/3 cup Homemade Caramel Sauce

1. Preheat the oven to 375°F.

2. In a medium saucepan, combine the apples, brown sugar, flour, butter, cinnamon, lemon juice, and salt. Cook on medium heat until slightly softened, stirring constantly.

3. Stir in ¾ cup Homemade Caramel Sauce. Stir until melted.

4. Pour the apple mixture onto the Sticky Toffee Pudding Filling in the piecrust.

5. Cover with Crumb Topping, lightly covering all of the pie filling.

6. Bake for 50 minutes or more, or until the pie filling bubbles over.

7. Cool on a rack and keep at room temperature.

8. When fully cooled, garnish with more Praline Pecans and Caramel Sauce.

Need a pie to impress the ladies? Women love layered pie, and my twin sister's is to-die-for delicious—along with Innovation Best in Show at the pie championships!

# Twin Blessings

I have always felt especially blessed to have my own best friend, my twin sister, Laura, by my side throughout my life. As children, we were together constantly—we ate, bathed, played, and slept together. We shared the same family, hobbies, and friends. And although we are fraternal twins, and look nothing alike, our shared childhood experiences formed a bond like no other.

I can still remember us walking hand in hand on our first day of kindergarten: up the tree-lined street two blocks and around the curve to our neighborhood school. I remember that Laura and I initially skipped up the street, feeling giddy and pretty in our new, matching dresses. However, as the school got closer, our gaits slowed, and we became more anxious about being separated. I remember squeezing her hand tight as we approached the school entrance, feeling pangs of sweet love and security that my twin, my best friend, was with me, that I was not alone. I also remember realizing that after school we would lock hands again and together walk happily home.

Life carries on, and at times thousands of miles have separated Laura and me. However, I will be forever comforted by that same feeling of sweet security that has remained in my heart all these years, no matter the distance between us. Our loved ones are always with us, a mere hand squeeze away in our memories. And someday we will walk happily hand in hand together all the way Home.

*Eat pie, love life.*

# Mommy's Boisterous Blackberry Raspberry Pie

## Eat pie, be thankful for sweet childhood memories.

When I was young my family would spend a week each summer camping up north at a spot overlooking Lake Michigan. The big lake was breathtakingly beautiful, but routinely ice cold. As kids, we didn't care and frolicked in the waves from dawn until dusk. One of the highlights of our week was going to Leland, a charming little village on the harbor. We would browse the unique shops and take home fresh-smoked whitefish, bread, and cheese. We would also stop at a local farm stand to pick up homegrown sweet corn, tomatoes, and sweet blackberries. Much as we enjoyed this outing, my brothers, sister, and I couldn't wait to get back to the campsite, for we knew we were in for a treat! You see, my mother was a master at outdoor cooking and no meal was more anticipated. We ate fried whitefish, fresh tomatoes, sweet corn, and the yummiest blackberry cobbler "pie" ever while enjoying a perfect Lake Michigan sunset.

**Recommended: Flaky Classic Piecrust, frozen (page 1), Sweetie-licious Crumb Topping (page 6)**

### Filling
5$^1$/$_2$ cups fresh or frozen blackberries
1 cup sugar
$^1$/$_4$ cup plus 1 tablespoon cornstarch
1 tablespoon fresh orange juice
2$^1$/$_2$ cups fresh or frozen raspberries

1. Preheat the oven to 375°F.

2. In a medium saucepan, combine the blackberries, sugar, and cornstarch.

3. Stir on medium heat until boiling.

4. Boil for 2 minutes, stirring constantly.

5. Remove from the heat. Add the orange juice.

6. Pour the fresh or frozen raspberries on the bottom of a frozen piecrust.

7. Top with the cooked blackberry filling.

8. Cover with Crumb Topping, covering all of the pie filling.

9. Bake for 50–60 minutes, or until the pie filling bubbles over.

10. Cool on a rack and keep at room temperature.

This pie won a first place for a reason—soooo good!

# Yankee Dixie Pie

Eat pie, be thankful for our veterans.

Without our veteran heroes, our American dream would not be. Let us remember them all, who made us the independent, democratic country we remain today. All of them, whether they are with us in body or spirit alone, deserve all the respect and recognition we, as Americans, can muster. But most important, they deserve our gratitude. Because without these heroes of America, we would not exist in the world that we know and, more than likely, take for granted every day.

So let us love, hug, give thanks, and pray for all living and passed veterans who carried out their heroic duties to make our lives peaceful, independent, equal, and safe, for the good of America and all humanity.

**Recommended: Sweetie-licious Cream Cheese Crust, frozen (page 2)**

**Filling**
1/2 cup butter, melted
1 cup brown sugar
1 tablespoon flour
1/8 teaspoon salt
3 eggs
1 teaspoon vanilla extract
1 cup whipping cream
1/2 cup finely chopped walnuts
1/2 cup chopped dates
1/2 cup coconut
1 cup dried tart cherries
1/4 cup mini chocolate chips

**Garnish—Optional**
Confectioners' sugar

1. Preheat the oven to 375°F.

2. In a medium bowl, combine the butter, brown sugar, flour, salt, eggs, and vanilla. Add the whipping cream and mix well.

3. Fold in the walnuts, dates, coconut, cherries, and chocolate chips.

4. Pour into a frozen piecrust and bake for approximately 50 minutes or until the center is set.

5. Let cool. Sprinkle with confectioners' sugar.

The old-fashioned sweet flavor of dates in this pie is a perfect pair with the dried tart cherries!

"Gratitude unlocks the fullness of life. . . . It can turn a meal into a feast, a house into a home, a stranger into a friend."
—Melody Beattie

# Chapter 4

# JOY

*"What a wonderful life I've had! I only
wish I'd realized it sooner."*

—Colette

I'm not sure there's anything more lovely than a joyful heart.
People with joyful hearts are like human magnets: Everyone is
immediately attracted to them. They bring a spirit to every situ-
ation that lifts the atmosphere to a happy calm. I think we all
can capture and spread more joy in our lives if we truly appreciate all our blessings every day. Think joy!

Our lives and pies must be bursting with joyful filling.

# Mom Hundt's Apple Almond Pie

Eat pie, love your children.

My husband, John, grew up in a family of thirteen children! His parents did a wonderful job raising them, ensuring that they all had charming childhoods, teaching virtues such as hard work, integrity, respect, faith, and love. John's mother was a wonderful cook and baker and insisted that all thirteen children had happy, celebrated birthdays. On their special day, each child was allowed to choose their favorite dinner for the evening, including their favorite dessert. My husband and his twin sister always chose the same birthday desserts year after year: Josie selected German chocolate cake, and it was all-American apple pie for John. (Clearly John was destined to be my husband, for he understood at an early age pie's allure and magnificence.) After dinner, much-anticipated birthday gifts were opened, balloons were passed out, and the whole family romped in the living room with smiling faces and contented bellies in magical "birthday land" euphoria.

**Recommended: Sweetie-licious Cream Cheese Crust, frozen (page 2)**

**Almond Filling**
1/4 cup plus 1 tablespoon sugar
1/2 cup plus 1 tablespoon almond paste, crumbled with fingers
1/4 cup butter, softened
1 cup flour
1/2 teaspoon salt
2 ounces cream cheese, softened

1. Using a pastry blender or fork in a medium bowl, combine the sugar, almond paste, butter, flour, and salt until the mixture is crumbly and fine.

2. Measure out 1 cup of this almond filling mixture to serve as a topping in a separate small bowl. Set aside.

3. Add the softened cream cheese to the remaining almond filling mixture, using your fingers to crumble it in until well mixed.

**Apple Filling**
6½ cups peeled, thinly sliced Michigan Cortland or Ida Red apples (5 medium-large)
1 cup sugar
1 teaspoon cinnamon
¼ teaspoon salt
2 tablespoons butter
1½ tablespoons flour
1 cup heavy whipping cream
¼ teaspoon almond extract

**Garnish**
2 tablespoons sliced almonds

1. Preheat the oven to 375°F.

2. In a large pan on medium heat, combine the apples, sugar, cinnamon, salt, butter, and flour. Stir constantly until the apples are just tender, approximately 10–15 minutes.

3. Add the whipping cream and stir for 5 more minutes.

4. Remove the pan from the stove and stir in the almond extract.

5. Crumble the almond filling into the bottom of a frozen piecrust.

6. Pour the apple filling on top of the almond filling.

7. Sprinkle with the reserved almond filling.

8. Bake for 50 minutes or until a knife slides easily into the center of the pie. During the last 5 minutes of baking, sprinkle on 2 tablespoons almonds for garnish.

You'll love this pie—the creamy almond layer mixed with apples is so amazingly delicious! Be sure to use a high-quality almond paste, as it makes a big difference.

# Betsie's Cool Key Lime Pie

## Eat pie, share in life's little excitements.

We are a pie-loving family and have celebrated birthdays with pies instead of traditional birthday cakes for generations. One year for my birthday, my husband decided to surprise me and make *me* my favorite key lime pie. He enlisted the "help" of our daughters, Ellie and Betsie, swearing the girls to secrecy on this special pie mission. The day before my birthday, as I set out grocery shopping for a few hours, John and the girls hurriedly made my birthday pie surprise, leaving not a trace of evidence. Upon my return, I was greeted at the door by all three of them bearing huge, suspicious smiles. The secret proved to be too much for sweet little Betsie, as she blurted out that my birthday pie was secretly made while I was out, and that it was going to be delicious! Of course, John and big sister Ellie were initially disappointed that their pact was broken so quickly. However, we all soon laughed wildly and we went on to celebrate my birthday—including the best key lime pie I have ever eaten, made with love.

**Recommended: Sweetie-licious Graham Cracker Crust (page 2)**

### Filling
28 ounces sweetened condensed milk
8 egg yolks
Zest of 2 limes
1 cup key lime juice
Dash of vanilla extract

### Garnish—Optional
Sweetie-licious Whipped Cream
   (see recipe on page 8)
Lime zest
White chocolate shavings

> "Whoever is happy, will make others happy too."
> —Anne Frank

1. Preheat the oven to 350°F.

2. Mix the condensed milk and egg yolks in a medium bowl. Add the lime zest, lime juice, and vanilla.

3. Pour into a pie shell and bake for 25 minutes or until the center is completely set.

4. Refrigerate for 3 hours.

5. Garnish with Whipped Cream, lime zest, and white chocolate shavings.

 I still have this pie for my birthday!

# Grandma Rosella's Lovely Lemon Meringue Pie

### Eat pie, take joy in life's little setbacks.

My father grew up during the Depression on a small farm in Michigan. Like most folks during that troubled time, they did not have much money. Fruit that didn't grow in your own backyard was considered special and hard to come by, so when my grandmother made lemon meringue pie, it was for special occasions only. One summer Sunday in 1937, Reverend Frye was scheduled to come to dinner at my father's farm. My grandmother awoke at dawn to make the special lemon pie. Years later, my father could still recall the sound of the fork clicking on the glass bowl while she whipped the egg whites into soft meringue clouds. After a few hours of baking, she set her lovely pie on the dining room window to cool while the family went off to church.

Unfortunately, Zip the beagle found the pie too much to resist. Upon the family's return, nothing was left of the beautiful pie but an empty pie pan and a contented dog sleeping with meringue stuck to his nose. Zip was sent to the barn from that day forward, and poor Reverend Fry never got to enjoy Grandma's pie. The sweet part of this saga is that the story has been told year after year at family gatherings, evoking joyful laughter each and every time. It solidifies the notion that sometimes, all we can do is . . . laugh!

**Recommended: Sweetie-licious Cream Cheese Crust, frozen (page 2)**

1. Preheat the oven to 375°F.

2. Line a frozen piecrust with one layer of aluminum foil and fill with one layer of uncooked pasta.

3. Bake in the oven until the bottom of the crust is light brown, approximately 25 minutes.

4. Carefully lift the foil from the crust. Let the crust cool.

5. Continue with the filling instructions below.

### Filling

1½ cups plus 2 tablespoons sugar
¼ cup cornstarch, sifted
⅛ teaspoon salt
1½ cups water
1 cup fresh lemon juice, strained
    from 3–4 lemons
2 teaspoons grated lemon zest
4 large egg yolks
½ teaspoon vanilla extract
2 tablespoons unsalted butter, cut
    into small pieces

In a large saucepan on medium heat, combine all of the ingredients and cook, whisking constantly, until the mixture boils and thickens. Pour into a piecrust.

### Meringue

1½ cups egg whites
½ teaspoon cream of tartar
¼ teaspoon lemon extract
¼ teaspoon vanilla extract
¾ cup sugar

1. In a medium mixing bowl using a handheld or stand mixer, beat the egg whites, cream of tartar, and lemon and vanilla extracts on medium speed until soft peaks form.

2. Gradually add the sugar, a few tablespoons at a time, beating on high speed until stiff glossy peaks form.

3. Immediately spread the meringue over the pie, sealing the edges of the crust to prevent shrinkage.

4. Bake for 7 minutes or until light brown.

 Fresh lemon juice and zest are musts in this pie!

You may need to turn the pie for even browning.

# John's Perfect Fresh Peach Blueberry Pie

*Eat pie, find wondrous joy in all things.*

I remember the first time I saw my husband, John. We were in our high school cafeteria line, and I decided he was so cute I had to flirt with him. After an awkward one-sided conversation, I realized that he either wasn't interested in me or was painfully shy. He was the latter. Besides his good looks, I find three things to be most endearing about him: his rock-solid work ethic, his tremendous family values, and the way he sees the world with joyful wonder. John's joy in nature is soulful, as he relishes every sunset, autumn leaf, and homegrown peach. His love for Christmas is also legendary, as each and every Christmas bulb, ornament, and gift is placed or purchased with tender thoughtfulness. But it is John's appreciation for desserts, especially pie, that always brings excitement to our family's kitchen table. His face lights up at every bite!

**Recommended: Flaky Classic Piecrust, frozen (page 1), Sweetie-licious Crumb Topping (page 6)**

**Filling**
5 cups peeled, sliced fresh in-season peaches
1 cup sugar
1/4 cup plus 1 tablespoon tapioca (minute variety)
1 teaspoon fresh lemon juice
1/2 teaspoon orange zest
1/4 teaspoon almond extract
1/2 cup fresh blueberries

1. Preheat the oven to 375°F.

2. In a large mixing bowl, combine the peaches, sugar, tapioca, lemon juice, orange zest, and almond extract. Stir until well mixed.

3. Let stand for 10 minutes or until the tapioca is softened to the touch, being watchful of time—you don't want the peaches to sit too long as the filling will be soupy.

4. Gently mix the fresh blueberries with the peaches and pour into a frozen piecrust.

5. Cover with Crumb Topping, covering all of the pie filling. Be especially generous around the edges.

6. Bake for 50–60 minutes, or until the filling bubbles over. Best eaten on the first day.

To bring out zingy, yummy fruit flavors, use citrus anything! Try orange, lemon, and lime juices or zests for more flavor pop.

# Summer's Frozen Creamy Strawberry & Lime Pie

## Eat pie, cherish the joys of summer in your soul.

I have many perfect summer memories from my childhood: hot summer nights when all five of us kids would hover around the living room floor fan, trying to keep cool while wailing nonsense noises into the fan's soft breeze; endless bicycle rides with my twin sister and friends, destination unknown; best of all, the faint melodic tune of the ice-cream truck and how our hearts raced as the tune became louder when it approached our home. And how excited we kids would get when our mom gave us each a quarter to get something cold and icy. I remember the pure summer bliss of sucking on an ice-cold Popsicle on our front porch in the scorching heat. The flavor combination of frozen lime and strawberry is also absolutely unforgettable in a pie! The cooled contentment will certainly take you back to the simple loves of yesteryear.

**Recommended: Sweetie-licious Graham Cracker Crust (page 2)**

**Filling**
1 (8-ounce) package cream cheese, softened
1 (14-ounce) can sweetened condensed milk
$1/2$ teaspoon vanilla extract
$1/2$ teaspoon almond extract
$1/3$ cup fresh squeezed lime juice (2–3 limes)
Zest of 2 fresh limes, divided
1 quart fresh in-season strawberries, washed, hulled, and slightly crushed, sweetened with
$3/4$ cup sugar, or to taste, OR
1 large package frozen sweetened strawberries, thawed

1. In a large mixing bowl, beat the softened cream cheese until creamy. Gradually add the sweetened condensed milk, vanilla and almond extracts, lime juice, and half the lime zest.

2. Pour into a crust. Freeze for at least 4 hours.

3. Mix the strawberries, sugar, and remaining lime zest. Refrigerate. If you're using frozen strawberries, omit the sugar.

4. Take the pie from the freezer, slice it into individual pieces, and ladle strawberries on top.

5. Keep the pie frozen.

 Super easy and refreshing—crushed fresh strawberries make this wonderful.

> "All succeeds
> with people who
> are sweet and
> cheerful."
> —Voltaire

# The Cutest Little Pie Shop
## in the Whole Wide World

My dream of owning a pie shop evolved on my Cape Cod honeymoon, when my husband and I stumbled upon a darling pie shop in one of the quaint villages. I was immediately smitten with the scurry of the bakers, the aroma of cinnamon, and the pies lined neatly in cases. I was enchanted . . . and enamored with the thought of creating my own little shop, retro-adorable, pink, and full of love!

I kept this sentiment close to my heart for over twenty years, dreaming of how cute it would someday be. I started gathering old tables, chairs, pie safes, dishes, and pink doilies at garage sales and stored them in our barn. I also honed my pie-baking skills, perfecting a collection of delicious pies for my family and friends to enjoy, with the hope of my customers someday enjoying them as well.

Patience and perseverance always pay off, as one cold November day in 2005, Sweetie-licious, the cutest little pie shop in the whole wide world, was born! Spices, Sinatra, and love suffused the little bakery. Cases were filled with dreamy cream pies and bursting fruit pies, all lined up in rows and ready for the world to finally enjoy. Everything was as I had dreamed of, right down to pink bakery boxes!

Today, thousands and thousands of pies and customers later, it has become the destination pie shop I knew it could be. It warms my heart to know how my pies have made so many folks' birthdays, holidays, and everyday dinners delightful, weddings unforgettable, and celebrations memorable. I love that people from all over the country come to soak in the nostalgia, the delicious homemade fare, and the experience of an old-fashioned pie shop.

To this day, when I walk in the front door, I am mesmerized and humbled by its pie magic. For it is, indeed, the cutest little pie shop in the whole wide world!

## Eat pie, love life.

# Linda's Cheery Chocolate Peppermint Cream Pie

## Eat pie, be happy with your thoughtful decisions.

In my childhood, my family would occasionally stop for lunch after church at a neighborhood Big Boy diner. When my daddy pulled into their parking lot, all of us kids went crazy with excitement, because eating out was a rare and special treat. Of course, there were rules about what we were allowed to order from the menu, ensuring that costs were kept to a minimum for our big family. We all understood and were grateful to be there. The choice was usually between a cheeseburger and a dessert— only one. For my siblings, this was a difficult decision, but not for me. Desserts were then, and continue to be, a major love of my life. I always chose pie, chocolate cream pie precisely. I loved its flaky crust, chocolaty, creamy filling, and the homemade whipped cream topping. I never once regretted my sensible, delicious decision, and make similar decisions to this day!

**Recommended: Sweetie-licious Chocolate Graham Cracker Crust (page 3)**

**Filling**
2 1/2 cups whole milk
3/4 cup half-and-half
4 egg yolks
1 cup sugar
1/4 cup brown sugar
1/4 cup plus 2 tablespoons cornstarch, sifted
1/3 cup Hershey's cocoa, sifted
1 1/2 teaspoons vanilla extract
1/2 teaspoon peppermint extract

**Garnish—Optional**
Sweetie-licious Whipped Cream (see recipe on page 8)
Crushed candy canes or peppermint candies
Chocolate shavings

1. Preheat the oven to 375°F.

2. Mix the milk, half-and-half, egg yolks, sugars, cornstarch, and cocoa in a medium saucepan.

3. Cook on medium heat, stirring constantly until the mixture boils for 1 minute.

4. Remove from the heat and add the vanilla and peppermint extracts.

5. Pour the filling into a piecrust and refrigerate for at least 3 hours.

6. Garnish with Whipped Cream and crushed candy canes, peppermint candies, or chocolate shavings.

# Ellie's Cherry Blackberry Peach Pie

*Eat pie, speak joy from the heart.*

When my daughter Ellie was a baby, my parents would babysit her a few days a week, which was a highlight for all involved. Because Ellie was their first grandchild, they lived for their "grandpa-ma days" and spoiled her. At Grandma's house, when most babies were eating baby food, my Ellie was eating pie. My mother would make special pie filling for her when she first started eating solid food, and as she grew, so did her pie palate. My daddy loved to tell of a time when Ellie was in her high chair, all ready for breakfast, and he asked what she wanted to eat. According to him, her whole sweet face was smiling as she uttered her very first word, "Pie!" Although she is all grown up now, it is still one of Ellie's favorite words—and mine too!

**Recommended: Flaky Classic Piecrust, frozen (page 1), Sweetie-licious Crumb Topping (page 6)**

### Filling
6 cups frozen tart cherries
1 cup bite-size-cut frozen peaches
1 cup sugar
1/4 cup cornstarch, sifted
1/2 teaspoon orange zest
1 1/2 cups frozen blackberries

1. Preheat the oven to 350°F.

2. Mix the cherries, peaches, sugar, and cornstarch in a medium saucepan.

3. Stir constantly on medium heat until the mixture is thick and boiling. Boil for 1 minute, constantly stirring.

4. Remove from the heat and add the orange zest.

5. Place blackberries on the bottom of a frozen pie shell. Pour the cherry mixture over the blackberries.

6. Cover with Crumb Topping, covering all of the pie filling.

7. Bake for 45–60 minutes or until the pie filling bubbles over.

Frozen fruit works perfectly in pies, as long as you follow the recipe carefully to make sure you add the right amount of thickeners, citrus zests, juices, and extracts to bring out the joyful taste of fruits.

# Daddy's County Fair Candy Apple Pie

## Eat pie, love food!

My father had an excellent memory and loved sharing his treasure trove of stories with all five of us kids. The heat of July always took him back to his boyhood summers on the farm during the 1930s and '40s, and he would reminisce about the summertime chores, the farm animals, and the beloved county fair. Fair week was the event of the summer back then, and something families eagerly looked forward to. He and my grandparents would take in the fair for hours on a Saturday evening, enjoying the exhibition halls filled with breads, pies, flower arrangements, and fast-talking salesmen showing off the latest and greatest gadgets and appliances. He also spoke of livestock barns filled with squeaky-clean pigs, cows, and chickens as well as hardworking farm kids hoping for blue ribbons. The carnival rides and games were of course colorful, fun, and flashy, with lots of dolled-up teenagers standing about. But the highlight, he said, was the fair food: steamed hot dogs, hand-dipped ice-cream cones, hot and crispy french fries, and his favorite, the sweet candy apples. The farm had a few apple trees, but my grandmother did not have time, money, or inclination to make anything but applesauce and pies. So my father's precious fair change was spent on something special and unique—the juicy, spicy cinnamon apple that he loved so much and fondly recalled his whole life. I created this pie recipe just for him.

**Recommended: Flaky Classic Piecrust, frozen (page 1), Sweetie-licious Crumb Topping (page 6)**

### Filling
6 1/2 cups peeled, small-diced Michigan Cortland or Ida Red apples (5 medium–large)
3/4 cup sugar
1 tablespoon flour
1/4 teaspoon salt
1/2 teaspoon fresh-squeezed lemon juice

**Candy Mixture**
1/3 cup red-hot candies
2 tablespoons cornstarch, sifted
1 tablespoon butter
1 cup water
1/8 teaspoon vanilla extract

1. Preheat the oven to 375°F.

2. Mix the apples, sugar, flour, salt, and lemon juice. Set aside.

3. Combine the red-hot candies, cornstarch, butter, water, and vanilla extract, stirring over medium heat in a medium saucepan until the candies are dissolved and the mixture is thickened.

4. Pour the candy mixture over the apple mixture. Combine well.

5. Pour into a frozen piecrust and lightly top with Crumb Topping.

6. Bake for 1 hour or until a knife goes through the middle of the pie smoothly.

When you're baking with apples and rhubarb, be sure to test their doneness by poking a knife through the middle of the pie. The knife should slide through easily. Then you know you have a deliciously baked pie!

Chapter 5

# WORK ETHIC

*"I have studied the lives of great men and famous women, and I found that men and women who got to the top were those who did their jobs in hand, with everything they had of energy and enthusiasm and hard work."*

—Harry Truman

I believe in my heart that a strong and grateful work ethic is one of the secrets to life. My lineage is from a long and strong line of farmers, school-teachers, and cooks—all professions that demand hard work to be successful. I also know that a solid work ethic is admirable and productive, as long as it is balanced with a harmonious family life. I believe that producing something worthy every day ignites your soul. Whether you are writing a report, plowing a field, cleaning your house, or making a pie—making each day count with passionate hard work, kind notions, and a grateful heart allows your head to rest peacefully each and every night.

There is no doubt about it: Creating a rewarding life or a glorious pie takes perseverance and hard work, but it is so worth the admirable efforts, for you, and for all you share your life with!

# Aunt Ruby's Beautiful Butterscotch Praline Pie

Eat pie, work hard at all you do.

My hardworking aunt Ruby lived at the bottom of a hill in beautiful West Virginia. She had magnificent gardens and orchards and canned everything from tangy watermelon pickles to sweet molasses. When my family came to visit, she was always the humble hostess, as we admired all of the work she put into her gardens, quilts, and canning cellar. But to me the highlight of our visit was the homemade dinner served on all of her best china—pickles of every sort, green beans and corn, biscuits with homemade apple butter, and delicious chicken and dumplings. Of course, my favorite was dessert, usually  her creamy butterscotch pie! The flaky crust, creamy filling, and crunchy pecans made for a perfect pie. Aunt Ruby worked hard all of her sweet life and was very proud of all that she accomplished. Her work ethic and passion for life are true tenets to live by.

**Recommended: Flaky Classic Piecrust, frozen (page 1)**

1. Preheat the oven to 375°F.

2. Line a frozen piecrust with one layer of aluminum foil and fill with one layer of uncooked pasta.

3. Bake in the oven until the bottom of the crust is light brown, approximately 25 minutes.

4. Carefully lift the foil from the crust. Let the crust cool.

5. Continue with the filling instructions below.

**Filling**
6 tablespoons butter
1 1/2 cups brown sugar
3/4 cup water
2 cups whole milk
3 egg yolks
Dash of salt
1/4 cup plus 1 tablespoon cornstarch

1 teaspoon vanilla extract
1/2 teaspoon artificial brandy—optional

**Garnish—Optional**
Sweetie-licious Whipped Cream (see recipe on page 8)
Sweetie-licious Praline Pecans (see recipe on page 6)

1. Melt the butter on low heat until browned, watching carefully so it doesn't burn.

2. Remove from the heat. Stir in the brown sugar and add the water slowly, so it doesn't splatter.

3. Return to the burner and turn up the heat to medium high. Whisk aggressively until the mixture boils.

4. Let it boil for 1 minute, stirring constantly, then remove the pan from the heat.

5. In a separate bowl, combine the milk, egg yolks, salt, and cornstarch until completely mixed.

6. Very slowly add this to butter-and-sugar mixture.

7. Return the mixture to medium-high heat until it boils. Boil for 1 minute stirring constantly.

8. Add the vanilla and brandy. Pour the mixture into a pie shell.

9. Cover with plastic wrap and refrigerate for at least 3 hours.

10. Garnish with Whipped Cream and Praline Pecans.

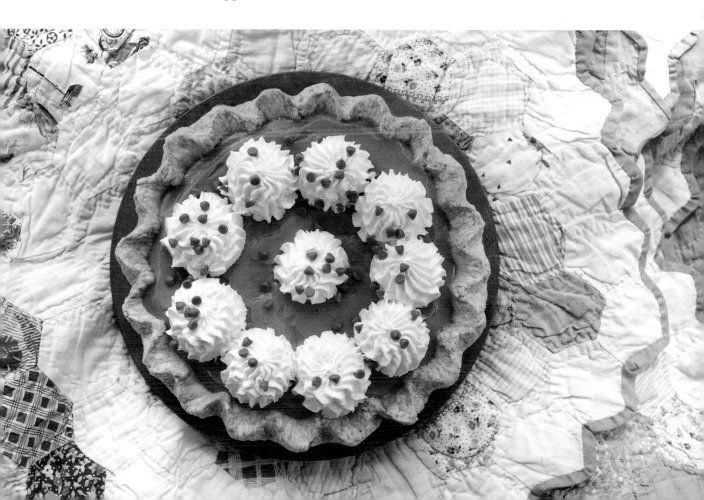

# Gail's Pretty Peach Rhubarb Pie

## Eat pie, love your work!

My dear friend and colleague Gail is one hard worker. As a retired librarian, she is wonderfully organized, sharp as a tack, and a loyal people pleaser. She washes our dishes, frames and hangs all of our media coverage for the shop's walls, and even skillfully manages our Facebook page and website. For all of her contributions to the shop, though, it's her piecrust-rolling skills that are probably the most revered! It was a gift from heaven the day she walked into my cute little pie shop and asked if I needed help rolling piecrusts. Thousands and thousands of crusts later, she joyfully leads our piecrust-rolling team each week as they make the flakiest and most tender crusts around. Gail's mother taught her to roll piecrusts at a very young age, and she has loved it  since. Gail is still working hard and doing what she loves—the secret to life! This pie is Gail's creation—her two favorite flavors in one pie.

Recommended: Flaky Classic Piecrust, frozen (page 1), Sweetie-licious Crumb Topping (page 6)

**Filling**

7 cups sliced frozen peaches, partially thawed
1¼ cups sugar
3 tablespoons cornstarch
¼ cup water
½ teaspoon almond extract
¼ teaspoon fresh orange zest
1 tablespoon butter
2 cups fresh or frozen rhubarb

1. Preheat the oven to 375°F.

2. Mix the peaches, sugar, cornstarch, and water in a medium pan on medium heat. Stir constantly until thickened.

3. Remove from the heat and add the almond extract, orange zest, and butter.

4. Place 2 cups rhubarb in a frozen piecrust. Pour the peach filling on top of the rhubarb.

5. Cover with Crumb Topping, covering all of the pie filling.

6. Bake for 50–60 minutes or until the filling bubbles over and a knife slides easily into the middle of the pie.

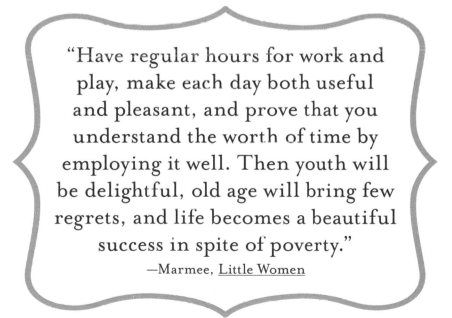

"Have regular hours for work and play, make each day both useful and pleasant, and prove that you understand the worth of time by employing it well. Then youth will be delightful, old age will bring few regrets, and life becomes a beautiful success in spite of poverty."
—Marmee, Little Women

# Aunt Margie's Raspberry & Cream Pie

## Eat pie, make yourself proud—of you!

While growing up in Michigan, my twin sister and I spent a much-anticipated week each summer at our dear aunt Margie's farm. Aunt Margie, a school-teacher, was naturally wonderful with children, and knew exactly what girls loved to do. We would go berry picking, help her can fruits and vegetables, help her wash clothes with the old-fashioned wringer washer, and even sew little aprons for ourselves and our dolls. However, the highlight of the week for us was certainly Saturday Baking Day.

We started baking at dawn in our aunt's tiny, pink kitchen to avoid the heat. We baked breads, cookies, and such, but pies were always my favorite, especially this one! My aunt tirelessly helped my sister and me make a perfect crust, a sweet raspberry filling, and finally the delicious cream filling. The day was long and tiring, but worth it all, for each summer the three of us consistently turned out beautiful raspberry pies. We couldn't wait for Uncle Howard to finally come home for supper, so we could show off our delicious masterpiece. This pretty pie is a sentimental favorite.

**Recommended: Sweetie-licious Cream Cheese Crust, frozen (page 2)**

1. Preheat the oven to 375°F.

2. Line a frozen piecrust with one layer of aluminum foil and fill with one layer of uncooked pasta.

3. Bake in the oven until the bottom of the crust is light brown, approximately 25 minutes.

4. Carefully lift the foil from the crust. Let the crust cool.

5. Continue with the filling instructions on next page.

**Raspberry Filling**
2 cups frozen raspberries
1 tablespoon cornstarch, sifted
1/4 cup sugar
1/4 teaspoon fresh lemon juice

**Cream Filling**
2 1/2 cups whole milk
3/4 cup half-and-half
4 egg yolks
1 1/4 cups sugar
1/3 cup cornstarch, sifted
1/8 teaspoon salt
1/2 teaspoon vanilla extract
1/2 teaspoon almond extract

**Garnish—Optional**
Sweetie-licious Whipped Cream (see recipe on page 8)
White chocolate shavings
Fresh raspberries

> "It is working
> which gives flavor
> to life."
> —Amiel

1. Mix the frozen raspberries, cornstarch, sugar, and lemon juice on medium-low heat in a small pan until thick, stirring constantly to prevent scorching. Set aside to cool.

2. Mix the milk, half-and-half, egg yolks, sugar, cornstarch, and salt together in a medium saucepan over medium heat. Stir constantly with a wire whisk until the mixture boils for 1 minute.

3. Remove from the heat. Stir in the vanilla and almond extracts.

4. Spread the cooled raspberry mixture into a piecrust until you can no longer see the bottom of the crust.

5. Pour the cream filling over the raspberry layer.

6. Cover with plastic wrap and refrigerate for at least 3 hours.

7. Garnish with Whipped Cream, white chocolate, and fresh raspberries.

# Aprons

One of my dear aunt Margie's favorite colors was pink, and she "simply pinked" almost everything around her. As a child I loved this, for she had a pink kitchen countertop, a pink bathroom, and a pink chenille bedspread! She also had several pink aprons for various cooking or baking situations. For everyday cooking she wore her simple flour sack aprons, but because she was a master seamstress she made even the most benign clothes adorable. Her daily home-keeping aprons were also decorated with pinkness—buttons, rickrack, and bows. Some even had bells attached, for fun.

Her hostess aprons were mostly pink, but she did add other colors for contrast. They were made with organza, tulle, or felt and adorned with big bows and sequins. These were to be worn for company only, although she did let my twin sister and me play dress-up with them when we came to visit. She even had children's aprons in plenty of pink and blue, just our size. It was always so much fun to cook and bake with her when we wore our special little aprons!

As I write these memories of my aunt, I realize why aprons are so special. Of course, their primary purpose is to prevent clothes from being soiled, but they have much greater meaning than that. Aprons bond cooking and fashion into one lovely piece of clothing. When you don a darling apron, you are intentionally celebrating the love and tradition of cooking and baking. And best of all, you will look absolutely lovely making a meat loaf and/or throwing a pie in the oven for your family and friends.

*Eat pie, love life.*

# West Virginia Honey Pie

Eat pie, work as hard as a honeybee!

While I was growing up, my family would spend a few weeks each summer in West Virginia, visiting my maternal grandparents. Their farm was on a mountaintop, with barns, chickens, gardens, acres of forest, and a swift creek running through. My grandpa was a retired coal miner who enjoyed his golden years tooling around his vegetable gardens, hunting, and caring for his bees. The beehives were set out by the barn, under an old silver maple tree a few hundred yards away from the house. Although I was scared of them, I was also mesmerized at the sound and deliberate activity of the bees as they worked in and out of the hives. My daddy always claimed that we all should work as hard as honeybees, as he too kept bees as a teenager during World War II.

Grandma would make pans of corn bread for breakfast and dinner, and I would happily drown my corn bread with Grandpa's golden wildflower honey, infused with pieces of chewy honeycomb in every bite. I created this pie recipe in memory of those summer days.

**Recommended: Flaky Classic Piecrust, frozen (page 1)**

1. Preheat the oven to 375°F.
2. Line a frozen piecrust with one layer of aluminum foil and fill with one layer of uncooked pasta.
3. Bake in the oven until the bottom of the crust is partially baked, approximately 8 minutes.
4. Carefully lift the pasta-filled foil from the crust.
5. Continue with the directions for the filling below.

**Filling**
4 eggs
2 egg yolks
2/3 cup honey—preferably wildflower, buckwheat, or clover
1 tablespoon butter, melted
1/2 teaspoon vanilla extract
Zest of 1 lemon
1/8 teaspoon salt
2 1/2 cups half-and-half
1 tablespoons plus 2 teaspoons cornstarch, sifted

**Garnish—Optional**
Fresh or frozen sweetened raspberries
Confectioners' sugar

1. Preheat the oven to 350°F.

2. Whisk the eggs and egg yolks in a medium bowl.

3. Add the honey, butter, vanilla, lemon zest, and salt and continue to mix thoroughly.

4. In a separate bowl, whisk the half-and-half and cornstarch until well mixed.

5. Mix into the honey mixture.

6. Pour into the piecrust.

7. Bake for 50 minutes or until the center is set. Cool on a rack and keep at room temperature.

8. Before serving, add a ladle of fresh or frozen sweetened raspberries over each slice. Powder the edges of the pie with confectioners' sugar right before serving.

I absolutely love this pie with orange blossom honey!

# Linda's Best Browned Butter Coconut Chess Pie

## Eat the best pie, love life!

I could talk pie for hours with Terry, a former colleague, friend, and fellow ardent pie lover. We discussed everything pie: cream pies versus fruit, canned cherries versus fresh, crumb topping versus lattice, meringue or not, and on and on. He wasn't very picky about his pies, which is where we disagreed immensely. My thoughts were, and continue to be, that if a pie isn't amazing, then I'm not interested. Terry, on the other hand, believed there to be only two kinds of pie: good pie and better pie! This always makes me smile and may be true for many readers. But for me, the only pie worth eating is the best pie.

I am quite certain that it's the experience of eating average pies over the years that has led me to my destiny. This is why I have a pie shop, ship pies, teach baking classes, and perform pie demonstrations across the country. I want to share what I have learned to ensure no one settles for a good pie, or even a better pie. I want everyone to have only the best pie. I have always said, if I can make a pie close to as good as your favorite pie baker, than I have done my job.

This pie is so yummy warmed up and served with butter pecan ice cream!

**Recommended: Sweetie-licious Cream Cheese Crust, frozen (page 2)**

1. Preheat the oven to 375°F.

2. Line a frozen piecrust with one layer of aluminum foil and fill with one layer of uncooked pasta.

3. Bake in the oven until the bottom is partially baked, approximately 8 minutes.

4. Carefully lift the pasta-filled foil from the crust. Let the crust cool.

5. Continue with the directions for the filling below.

**Filling**
3/4 cup butter
3/4 cup sugar
3/4 cup brown sugar
1 1/2 cups coconut, toasted
4 eggs
3/4 cup heavy cream

1/2 teaspoon almond extract
1/2 teaspoon vanilla extract
1 tablespoon flour

**Garnish—Optional**
Toasted coconut
Confectioners' sugar

1. Preheat the oven to 350°F.

2. Melt the butter on low heat until it's browned, watching carefully so it doesn't burn. Let it cool for 10 minutes.

3. Combine the browned butter, sugar, brown sugar, and eggs in a large bowl and whisk until smooth.

4. Add the remaining ingredients and combine until well mixed.

5. Pour into the piecrust and bake for 45 minutes or until the pie is set in the middle. Cool.

6. Dust the edges of the pie with toasted coconut and confectioners' sugar right before serving, if desired.

# Dad Hundt's Maple Chocolate Swirl Pie

Eat pie, make your family feel special.

My husband's father was a master carpenter and proud father of thirteen children. He worked six days a week his whole life and loved building beautiful, sound homes. He was always willing to go the extra mile to see that his best work was his only work. Dad Hundt felt blessed to have the life he had, and worked hard to make sure his family was raised with values of faith and love. John and his siblings loved him dearly and, like most kids, couldn't wait until he came home at night, through the back door and directly down the stairs to take off his work boots and coat, then put away his lunch box. With this, five or six of the younger kids would scurry down to welcome him home with hugs and laughter. The tradition was  for him to gather his beloved kids in his arms, and on his back, as he gingerly and joyfully walked up the stairs to a delicious homemade dinner. My father-in-law loved anything sweet, and my mother-in-law, a fantastic baker, would make her family delicious cakes, cookies, and pies every day to show her love.

**Recommended: Sweetie-licious Cream Cheese Crust, frozen (page 2)**

1. Preheat the oven to 375°F.
2. Line a frozen piecrust with one layer of aluminum foil and fill with one layer of uncooked pasta.
3. Bake in the oven until the bottom of the crust is light brown, approximately 25 minutes.
4. Carefully lift the foil from the crust. Let the crust cool.
5. Continue with the filling instructions on next page.

**Filling**
2 cups half-and-half
1 cup whole milk
1/2 cup maple syrup
4 egg yolks
1 cup brown sugar
1/3 cup plus 1 teaspoon cornstarch, sifted
1/8 teaspoon salt
3/4 teaspoon maple flavoring
1 teaspoon vanilla extract
1 ounce (2 squares) sweetened baking chocolate, melted

**Garnish—Optional**
Sweetie-licious Whipped Cream (see recipe on page 8)
Chocolate shavings
Maple sugar candies

1. Mix the half-and-half, milk, maple syrup, egg yolks, brown sugar, cornstarch, and salt in a medium pan.

2. Cook on medium heat, stirring constantly, until the mixture boils and thickens. Add the maple flavoring and vanilla.

3. Reserve 1 cup of filling in a separate medium bowl.

4. Add the melted chocolate to the reserved filling and mix until smooth.

5. Pour the chocolate filling into the bottom of a piecrust.

6. Whisk the remaining filling until smooth. Pour on top of the chocolate filling.

7. Take a spoon and lift the bottom layer of chocolate filling to the top and swirl. Repeat once. Stop yourself from continuing to swirl or you will end up with a muddy-looking pie.

8. Cover with plastic wrap and refrigerate for at least 3 hours. Garnish to taste with Whipped Cream, chocolate shavings, or maple sugar candies, if desired.

# Chapter 6

# PASSION

*"What is passion? It is surely the becoming of a person."*

—John Boorman

Passion is the spark in our soul that keeps our lives ignited with love and interest. Finding our passions is quite easy, as they are the things in our lives that we love to do, see, make, create, and be! Passion gives our lives purpose and allows our true souls to be exposed to our individual earthly delights. Having passions is a blessing and another secret to life. I believe that our own personal passions allow us to bring others happiness through what we have earned, learned, and loved.

Our lives, like an amazing pie, must be filled with passion—full of flavor and excitement!

# Laura & Linda's Holiday Eggnog Pie

## Eat pie, keep holiday traditions.

Our family, like most families, had a few essential holiday traditions that we all cherished: holiday baking, midnight church service, watching Christmas television specials, cutting down the Christmas tree, and our love for eggnog! I can still see all five of us kids watching with excitement as my mom poured the creamy eggnog into our special Santa mugs, ensuring that we all had the same amount of the liquid gold. She would garnish each with freshly grated nutmeg, making them taste over-the-top Christmas delicious!

I remember a few times when the eggnog was so rich and thick, my twin sister and I would get tummy aches from drinking it too fast. We never cared, though, because this Christmas tradition was too delicious to pass up. Now that we each have our own families, eggnog is still part of our family tradition, a must-have at every holiday gathering.

**Recommended: Sweetie-licious Cream Cheese Crust (page 2)**

**Filling**
2¹/2 cups milk
³/4 cup half-and-half
5 egg yolks
1¹/4 cups sugar
¹/3 cups cornstarch, sifted
Dash of salt
1 tablespoon butter
1 teaspoon vanilla extract
¹/2 teaspoon freshly grated nutmeg

**Garnish—Optional**
Freshly grated nutmeg
Sweetie-licious Whipped Cream (see
    recipe on page 8)
White chocolate shavings

1. In a medium saucepan over medium heat, whisk together the milk, half-and-half, egg yolks, sugar, cornstarch, and salt. Stir constantly until the mixture boils and thickens for 1 minute.

2. Remove from the heat. Whisk in the butter, vanilla, and fresh nutmeg until well mixed.

3. Immediately pour the cream mixture into a piecrust. Cover with plastic wrap and refrigerate for at least 3 hours.

4. Garnish to taste with freshly grated nutmeg, Whipped Cream, and white chocolate shavings.

# Aunt Ella's Cherry Berry Berry Pie

## Eat pie, live well.

My great-aunt Ella called Northern Michigan her home for nearly ninety years. As a schoolteacher, she spent her summers baking at an inn located on the shores of beautiful Lake Michigan and across the road from a cherry orchard: a perfect combination for breathtaking views and fresh, homemade cherry pies. Tourists would line up for hours to take in dinner, a golden sunset, and a piece of my aunt's heavenly pie.

My aunt loved her life, inspiring both students in the classroom and pie lovers at the inn year after year. Unfortunately, time does not stand still, for the inn and my sweet aunt are both long gone. Thankfully, Aunt Ella's cherished pie recipe was passed down to me, and it has become an all-time customer favorite. Aunt Ella's passionate yet simple life was rich and full, a true testament that less is, indeed, more.

**Recommended: Flaky Classic Piecrust, frozen (page 1), Sweetie-licious Crumb Topping (page 6)**

**Filling**
1 cup sugar
1/4 cup cornstarch
6 cups frozen unsweetened pitted tart red cherries
1/2 teaspoon finely shredded lemon zest
1 teaspoon fresh lemon juice
1/2 teaspoon almond extract
1 1/2 cups frozen red raspberries
3/4 cup frozen blueberries

1. Preheat the oven to 375°F.

2. In a large saucepan, mix the sugar, cornstarch, and cherries. Gently toss until the cherries are coated.

3. Cook and stir constantly over medium heat until bubbly.

4. Remove from the heat. Stir in the lemon zest, lemon juice, and almond extract. Add the raspberries and blueberries, stirring gently.

5. Pour in a frozen pie shell. Cover with Crumb Topping, covering all of the pie filling. Bake for 50–60 minutes or until the pie filling bubbles over.

All fruit, chess, and nut pies should be stored at room temperature, on your kitchen counter—or possibly your bedroom nightstand, ready for an easy midnight snack!

# Grandma Ferrell's Caramel Apple Pie

## Eat pie, simply love what you do.

There was nothing our family enjoyed more than our summers at my grandparents' farm in West Virginia. The farm itself was a bit run-down, but beautiful to me, with plenty of flower and vegetable gardens and dozens of chickens running about. There was always plenty of fine storytelling, bluegrass music, and delicious, homegrown food to share at the farm.

I loved to watch my grandmother work magic in the kitchen. She was the head cook at the high school's cafeteria, and a master of her craft. She claimed that she started cooking before she started primary school and that no one ever turned away one of her meals. She was known all over the county for her ability to fix up wild game with fresh herbs and dandelion wine. Everything she made was simply delicious—her fried chicken, biscuits, and gravy were legendary, but her apple pie was my favorite. The filling was tart, yet sweet, with a crumb topping that was buttery with just the right amount of cinnamon. I can still remember sitting with Granny on her porch swing, peeling apples and listening to her tales of her sweet and passionate life.

If you don't feel like making homemade caramel, just be sure to buy good-quality caramel—it does make a big difference!

**Recommended: Flaky Classic Piecrust, frozen (page 1), Sweetie-licious Crumb Topping (page 6)**

### Apple Filling
7 cups peeled, small-diced Michigan Cortland or Ida Red apples (5 medium–large)
1/2 cup sugar
1/2 cup dark brown sugar
2 tablespoons flour
3 tablespoons butter, melted
1 1/2 teaspoons cinnamon
1 teaspoon lemon juice
1/4 teaspoon salt

### Garnish
1/3 cup Homemade Caramel Sauce (see recipe on page 7)

1. Preheat the oven to 375°F.

2. In a medium bowl, combine all of the apple filling ingredients. Let stand for 10 minutes. Pile the apple mixture high into a frozen pie shell.

3. Sprinkle with Crumb Topping just until the apples are covered.

4. Bake for 1 hour or until a knife easily slides into the center of the pie with no resistance.

5. Cool. Top with Caramel Sauce, heating in the microwave for 20 seconds or until the caramel drizzles easily onto the pie.

Don't forget salt—it is so important in all cooking and baking, as it brings out the flavor of foods.

# The Moms' Pumpkin Caramel Apple Pie

## Eat pie, be creative in all you do.

My mother and grandmother taught me the importance of traditions and modeled their love of cooking and baking for me through their delicious homemade foods. Thus, I have always loved the traditional holiday of Thanksgiving, both for its simple meaning of gratitude, and for the glorious food associated with it. I adore all Thanksgiving pies, and can never decide between my mother's pumpkin and my grandma's caramel apple. My solution to the dilemma is this pie, incorporating both pies' wondrous qualities. It has the classic, creamy pumpkin filling atop the timeless, caramel apple pie filling, a combination that completely satisfies your traditional taste buds with spice, creamy pumpkin, and tart apples all in one memorable crust. I love Franklin's famous quote, "Necessity is the mother of invention," as it surely has helped many worthy inventions be created, including this yummy pie!

**Recommended: Flaky Classic Piecrust, frozen (page 1)**

**Pumpkin Filling**
1¼ cups canned pumpkin
1 cup half-and-half
½ cup sugar
2 eggs, slightly beaten
1 tablespoon flour

2 teaspoons pumpkin pie spice
¼ teaspoon cloves
½ teaspoon orange zest
¼ teaspoon salt
1 teaspoon cinnamon

In a medium mixing bowl, combine the pumpkin filling ingredients until well mixed. Set aside.

**Apple Filling**
3 medium Cortland or Ida Red apples, peeled, thinly sliced, and diced
¼ cup sugar
1 tablespoon flour
1 tablespoon butter, melted

1 teaspoon cinnamon
½ teaspoon lemon juice
⅛ teaspoon salt
½ cup Homemade Caramel Sauce (see recipe on page 7)

**Garnish—Optional**
Sweetie-licious Whipped Cream (see recipe on page 8)
Dried apples
Homemade Caramel Sauce
Freshly grated nutmeg

1. Preheat the oven to 375°F.

2. In a medium saucepan, cook all of the apple filling ingredients except the Caramel Sauce on medium heat until the apples are almost cooked through. Add the Caramel Sauce and stir until melted. Remove from the stove.

3. Pour the apple filling into the bottom of a frozen piecrust. Cover with the pumpkin filling.

4. Bake for 45–60 minutes or until the middle of the pie quivers.

5. Garnish to taste with Whipped Cream, dried apples, and more Caramel Sauce, dusting with grated nutmeg.

Always use tart apples to counter the sweetness of the natural and added sugar in pies. Use firm apples to ensure that they don't break down like applesauce during the baking process! I personally use Michigan apples; Cortlands, Ida Reds, and Northern Spies are favorites. Granny Smiths work well too.

# Hill Sisters' Creamy Chicken Pie

## Eat pie, find the things that stir your soul!

Grandma Ferrell came from a family of sixteen children. She grew up in southern West Virginia in a mountain holler called Big Ugly. Her mother, my great-grandmother Hill, was a wonderful cook from necessity and passion! She taught all nine of her daughters how to bake delicious pies and cobblers, and how to cook an old rooster into a tender pot of chicken dumplings. My grandma and her sisters were quite passionate and competitive when it came to their cooking and were known to get in heated arguments regarding who made the best blackberry cobbler or chicken pie—even to the point of not speaking for months based on things that were said of one another's culinary masterpieces. I have eaten simply remarkable dinners at all their kitchen tables, and can attest they all have the magical touch. They were all wonderful hosts, passionate about how food tasted and its presentation, and they loved to make folks happy with their talents. This adaptation of my grandmother's chicken pie recipe is in honor of them all.

**Filling**
2 tablespoons butter
1 tablespoon olive oil
3 boneless chicken breasts, roughly cut
  and cooked
1 medium onion, thinly sliced
3 baby red potatoes, diced
2 teaspoons garlic salt, or to taste
2 tablespoons flour
1/2 teaspoon freshly ground pepper
1 teaspoon poultry seasoning
1/4 cup minced fresh thyme
1/2 cup white wine
2 1/4 cups chicken stock (not broth)
3/4 cup half-and-half
1 cup frozen peas and carrots, partially cooked
1 egg beaten with 1 teaspoon water

1. Preheat the oven to 375°F.

2. In a large frying pan over medium heat, melt the butter and olive oil. Add the chicken, onion, potatoes, and garlic salt; cook, stirring often, for 10 minutes or until the potatoes are cooked through.

3. Stir in the flour, pepper, poultry seasoning, and thyme. Pour in the wine.

4. Add the chicken stock and half-and-half; cook until the mixture thickens. Add the peas and carrots.

5. Pour the mixture into a deep-dish 9- or 10-inch pie pan. Place a crust on top of the chicken mixture and crimp it into the sides of the dish. Brush with egg wash and cut three slits in the top crust to release steam.

6. Bake for 30–40 minutes or until lightly browned.

Buy pre-grated cheese, rotisserie chicken, and even pre-washed and sliced fruit and vegetables to make sweet and savory pies easier to make for speedy, yummy dinners!

# Comfort Food

I just got back from a very filling and comforting meal at Bob Evans with my husband, daughters, and elderly parents. We all sat around eating and smiling while stuffing dinner roll after dinner roll smothered in butter and honey in our mouths. The meal was good and comforting, exactly what Mr. Evans was aiming for, I suspect.

Actually, the same exact scene takes place at my own dining room table three or four times a week as my family gathers to eat delicious, warm, and comforting food.

The trueness of comfort food is indisputable. We underestimate the sincerity of a platter of pork chops and homemade applesauce or the coziness of a pot of chicken and dumplings simmering on the back burner. Nothing beats the security of a warm cinnamon apple pie—nothing. Comfort food soothes our souls, makes us feel loved, revered, and significant. I propose that we all make our dinners as loving and comforting as possible with whatever foods hold true for our own individual families. Together, my sweeties, we will change the world one pie and tuna noodle casserole at a time.

*Eat pie, love life.*

"The future belongs to those who believe in the beauty of their dreams."
—Eleanor Roosevelt

# Mr. & Mrs. McComb's Pumpkin Cheesecake Praline Pie

## Eat pie, love people!

My parents are clearly people persons. They truly love people, and thoroughly enjoy talking to all who cross their path. The bank teller, waitress, and hardware store assistant all become fast friends for life, as my parents can find out someone's backstory in a matter of minutes. When we were growing up, Mom and Dad loved to have people to the house as well; anyone and everyone was welcome for dinner.

When Mormon missionaries knocked on our door, my parents invited them in, explained to them that they were devout Methodists, and asked them to stay for dinner. We had Mormon missionaries for dinner all of my teenage years, and it's a tradition I continue in my own home today.

When we had company for dinner, my mother usually made lasagna or a roasted chicken—with pie for dessert, of course! My parents were genuinely delighted in all people, and were quite the loving pair for almost sixty years. No matter your race, religion, social status, or sexual preference, if you were a human being, they liked you. What a legacy.

**Recommended: Sweetie-licious Cream Cheese Crust, frozen (page 2)**

**Cream Cheese Layer**
1 (8-ounce) package cream cheese, softened
1/4 cup brown sugar
1/4 teaspoon vanilla extract
1 egg

**Pumpkin Layer**
1 1/4 cups canned pumpkin
1 1/4 cups half-and-half
1 cup sugar
3 eggs, slightly beaten
2 teaspoons pumpkin pie spice
1/4 teaspoon cloves
1/4 teaspoon orange zest
1 teaspoon cinnamon
1/4 teaspoon salt
1/4 cup Sweetie-licious Praline Pecans
   (see recipe on page 6)

**Garnish—Optional**
Freshly grated nutmeg

1.  Preheat the oven to 375°F.

2.  In a medium bowl, combine the cream cheese, brown sugar, and vanilla until well mixed. Add the egg when all of the ingredients are well combined. Spread onto the bottom of the piecrust.

3.  Combine the pumpkin, half-and-half, sugar, eggs, pumpkin pie spice, cloves, orange zest, cinnamon, and salt until well mixed. Carefully pour over the cream cheese mixture. Swirl the cream cheese mixture in a spiral pattern into the pumpkin mixture.

4.  Sprinkle the Praline Pecans over the top of the pie.

5.  Bake for 50 minutes or until almost set in the middle. Cool. Dust with grated nutmeg.

 This pie freezes well.

# Chapter 7

# KINDNESS

*"Wherever there is a human being there is a chance for kindness."*

—Seneca

Of all my memories, the kind ones stand out as examples of how I want to live my life. What we do for others with a genuinely kind heart is a blessing to everyone—but most important to our own self, as a kind heart is the outcome of a loving soul. I can think of many times a kindhearted person made me feel worthy and important at a time when I was feeling unimportant and unworthy. If we decide to be kind in our everyday lives, we will undoubtedly see a difference in our own character, and how we feel about ourselves. And being kind in our words and actions influences others to do the same. For kindness is the magical core of love, faith, and gratitude.

There is nothing better on this earth than sharing a kind heart and a slice of delicious, homemade pie!

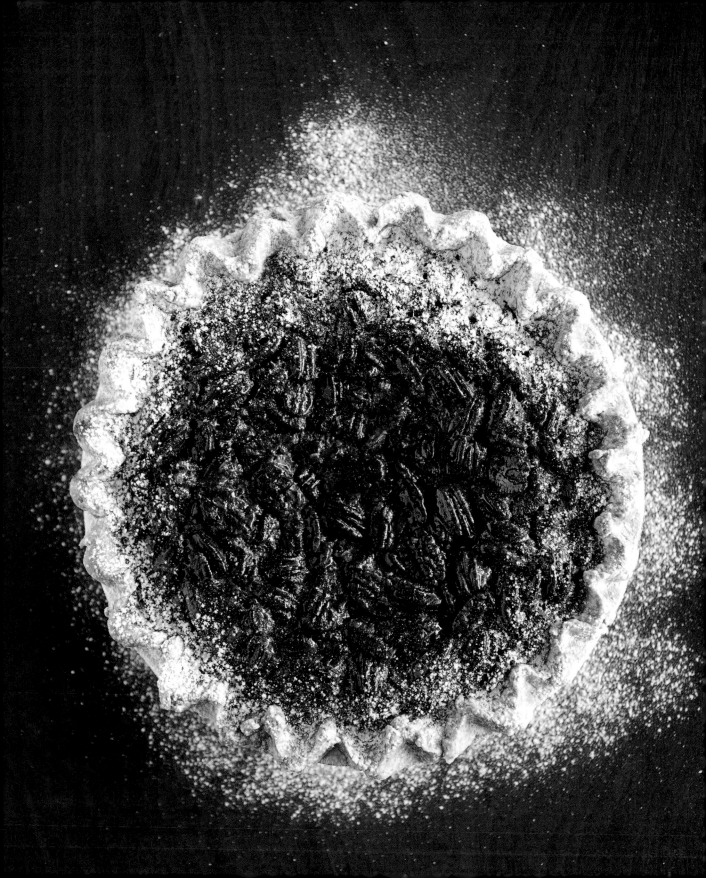

# Mrs. Cochran's Perfect Pecan Pie

## Eat pie, love your neighbors.

As I was growing up in Michigan, our family lived in an older, quaint neighborhood with mature trees and well-manicured lawns. Through the years neighbors would come and go, but there was one couple who made a lasting impression on all of us. The Cochrans were a worldly middle-aged couple with no children of their own. I am certain that our lively family of seven probably seemed hectic to the reserved pair, although I think they enjoyed our chaos. All of us children loved the Cochrans and relished any opportunity to be invited into their serene home to listen to travel stories and eat cinnamon candy. I remember one special day when Mrs. Cochran asked my sister and me into her sun-filled kitchen for a piece of pecan pie. She served the creamy pie on delicate bone china with beautiful lace napkins, both family heirlooms, making two little girls feel so loved and special.

Recommended: Flaky Classic Piecrust, frozen (page 1)

**Filling**
3 eggs
1/2 cup sugar
1/2 cup dark brown sugar
1/2 teaspoon salt
3 tablespoons butter, melted
3/4 cup dark corn syrup
1 tablespoon flour

1 cup whipping cream
1 teaspoon vanilla extract
2 tablespoons brandy
2 cups chopped or whole pecans

**Garnish—Optional**
Real maple syrup

1. Preheat the oven to 375°F.

2. In a medium mixing bowl, beat the eggs, sugars, salt, butter, corn syrup, flour and cream. Stir in the vanilla, brandy, and pecans. Pour into a frozen pie shell.

3. Bake for 45–60 minutes or until the filling is set. Cool.

4. Brush on maple syrup if desired.

The cream in this pie sets it apart!

# Lenora's Tomato Bacon Custard Pie

Eat pie, share the kindness.

At first glance I wasn't too impressed when my mother gave me my grandmother's old and worn cookbook. It seemed like a scrapbook filled with notes and recipes from newspapers, magazines, and the like. However, when I read the inscription letter that my grandmother wrote, I was filled with the warmth of a sweet friendship.

The cookbook had originally belonged to my grandmother's dear friend Lenora, and was shared by them. Their friendship started in the early 1940s, when my grandparents' farm didn't have electricity, but did have a washing machine. Her new neighbor, Lenora, had electricity but no washing machine. So, like all good friends and neighbors, they shared their blessings. Grandma hauled her wringer washing machine over to Lenora's back porch where each week they spent one whole day together, washing, ironing, cooking, and baking. They shared life's troubles and triumphs while making soups, casseroles, and pies. When my grandmother was sick, Lenora came over and canned all her beans before they spoiled, and made food for a week for Grandma's family. And they shared this cookbook, exchanging it back and forth, each adding recipes that struck their fancy.

When I opened up the cookbook and read the letters and food-spattered recipes, I got teary-eyed. I so understand the special bond that happens when folks cook together. Whether you are cooking or baking with your family, friends, or co-workers, life just becomes sweeter in the kitchen, especially when we cook for others! Grandma's notes say that Lenora taught her to make creamed tomatoes, which were the inspiration for this pie.

**Recommended: Flaky Classic Piecrust, frozen (page 1)**

### Crouton Topping
1 cup croutons, crushed using food
    processor or rolling pin
1 tablespoon butter, melted

Mix the ingredients together in a small bowl with a fork until crumbly. Set aside.

I love this pie for brunches and showers!

**Filling**

10 slices bacon, cooked and crumbled
1 tablespoon real maple syrup
1/2 cup chopped green onions
3 tomatoes, ripe and in season, cut into
    1/2-inch slices, and seeded (use your
    thumb to extract seeds)
1 cup grated swiss cheese

1 cup grated white cheddar cheese
1 1/2 cups half-and-half
2 eggs
1 teaspoon garlic salt
1/8 teaspoon pepper
1/2 teaspoon allspice
2 tablespoons white wine
1 teaspoon chopped fresh thyme

1. Preheat the oven to 375°F.

2. Mix the bacon with the maple syrup and sprinkle on the bottom of a frozen pie shell. Sprinkle the green onions over the bacon. Place the tomatoes over the bacon and onions. Sprinkle lightly with swiss and white cheddar cheeses.

3. Combine the half-and-half, eggs, garlic salt, pepper, allspice, wine, and fresh thyme in a medium bowl until mixed thoroughly.

4. Pour over the bacon-tomato filling, pressing down the filling so the egg mixture covers it completely.

5. Sprinkle with the crouton topping and bake for approximately 45–60 minutes or until the center is set.

# Faye's Sweetie Potato Pie

## Eat pie, be generous!

My dear friend Faye grew up in the 1950s and '60s in a small town in Texas. She has wonderful memories of her loving family and neighbors getting together for dancing, Motown music, and delicious southern comfort food. Clearly, food, fun, and folly were constants in Wichita Falls. Faye's mother was known for her sweet potato pies in particular, which were the best in town. Her pies were creamy and made with Texas sweet potatoes, with just the right amounts of nutmeg and butter.

When people started ordering her legendary pies for Thanksgiving, she baked for all who asked, charging no one for her efforts, for she considered the pies her gift to make. As more people heard about her sweet potato pies, her entire first floor transformed to a sea of pies every Thanksgiving eve. This lovely tradition went on for years, as she never could turn anyone away from one of her pie masterpieces, right up until the day she died. My friend Faye has such beautiful memories of her beloved mother: her sense of humor, her love for all things, and especially her generosity. Her mother understood the beauty of using your gifts, and giving back, and passed the legacy on to all who knew and loved her with this recipe.

**Recommended: Sweetie-licious Cream Cheese Crust, frozen (page 2)**

### Filling
2 pounds sweet potatoes, cooked, peeled, and mashed
4 large eggs
3/4 cup brown sugar
1/4 cup butter, melted

2 teaspoons vanilla extract
2 teaspoons nutmeg
1/2 teaspoon salt
1/4 teaspoon almond extract
1/2 teaspoon orange zest
1 cup half-and-half

1. Preheat the oven to 350°F.

2. In a large mixing bowl, using a handheld or stand mixer, combine the potatoes, eggs, brown sugar, and butter until well mixed. Add the vanilla, nutmeg, salt, almond extract, and orange zest; mix well. Add the half-and-half and mix well.

3. Pour into an frozen pie shell and bake for 45–60 minutes or until the middle is almost set.

I used fresh sweet potatoes, cooled and peeled, for this recipe, but you can substitute the same amount of canned yams.

# Farm Market Love

I absolutely love the magnetic atmosphere of farm markets and the steady commerce they have produced for centuries. The hustle and bustle of the satisfied vendors and customers, the aroma and beauty of the perfectly ripe fruits and vegetables, and the outdoor sunshine and breezes swirling in the pavilion or tents have a uniquely loving, comforting energy like nothing else.

I have such lovely memories of my daddy taking my twin sister and me downtown to the city farm market early on Saturday mornings. With a daughter on each hand, he would take us down the crowded aisles to buy his beloved vegetables and such; large pink radishes, fresh sweet corn, garden-ripe tomatoes, and local artisan Colby cheese were his staples. I enjoyed them all, but my favorite was the bakery booth stacked with various homemade breads and doughnuts, a delight for a sweet-toothed little girl to see. Because my father grew up on a farm, he had much appreciation for farmers and their bounty and loved visiting with his vendor friends. Listening to these conversations, I realized at a young age the importance not only of buying local, but more important of the emotional connection between people and food.

It seemed only natural for me to start selling my own pies at our local farm market when I first started my home-based business years ago. I will never forget the love in the air as my customers came to my vintage-tableclothed booth and bought me out week after week.

*Eat pie, love life.*

# Aunt Grace's Fresh Peaches & Cream Pie

## Eat pie, share with others.

When my mother was about seven, she remembers padding barefoot along a well-worn sandy path that connected her southern West Virginia farm to her aunt Grace's. Great-Aunt Grace lived in a weathered wooden structure flanked by two great pine trees, resting in a horseshoe of luscious green hills. In addition to the sweet scents of roses, phlox, and heliotrope, my mother remembers the delicious smell of freshly baked pies wafting from her aunt's kitchen window. Best of all, dear Aunt Grace lovingly welcomed my mother and always shared from her table. My mother can attest that her peach pie, unbeatable at the county fair, had the taste of heaven.

**Recommended: Flaky Classic Piecrust, frozen (page 1)**

1. Preheat the oven to 375°F.
2. Line a frozen piecrust with one layer of aluminum foil and fill with one layer of uncooked pasta.
3. Bake in the oven until the bottom of the crust is light brown, approximately 25 minutes.
4. Carefully lift the foil from the crust. Let the crust cool.
5. Continue with the filling instructions below.

**Filling**

2 1/2 cups whole milk
3 egg yolks
1 cup sugar
Dash of salt
1/4 cup cornstarch, sifted
1 tablespoon butter
1/4 teaspoon vanilla extract
1/8 teaspoon almond extract

1. Mix the milk, half-and-half, egg yolks, sugar, salt, and cornstarch in a medium pan. Cook on medium heat, stirring constantly until the mixture boils and thickens.
2. Remove from the heat. Add the butter and extracts.
3. Pour the filling into the piecrust and refrigerate for at least 3 hours.

**Fresh Peach Glaze**
2 cups sliced and mashed fresh peaches
1 cup sugar
1/2 cup water

1/4 cup cornstarch, sifted
1/4 teaspoon orange zest
1/4 teaspoon almond extract
4 cups sliced fresh peaches

1. Mix the sliced and mashed peaches, sugar, water, cornstarch, orange zest, and almond extract in a medium pan on medium heat until thickened. Chill until cold.

2. Place the fresh peach slices in a large bowl; add the peach glaze and stir until the slices are completely coated. Top the pie with the peach glaze. Best eaten on the first day. Keep refrigerated.

 Sweet in-season peaches are a must for this pie.

"Kind words can be short and easy to speak, but their echoes are truly endless."
—Mother Teresa

# Sharie's Summer Pink Lemonade Cream Pie

## Eat pie, share your talents.

My fellow baker and dear friend Sharie has many gifts. She is a wonderful cook and talented baker, has a great sense of humor, and completely lives out *simple abundance* as a way of being. But her greatest gift of all is her innate giving spirit. She truly understands that if you give of yourself, it will come back to you twofold. If anyone is in need, she is the first to their aid with a pie, a loaf of lemon bread, or pan of macaroni and cheese. Sharie's compassion for others has always been a joy to witness; as for her, doing for others fuels her joyful spirit like nothing else.

At the shop her sense of fun and her baking talents often spill into her giving heart, as she can create wonderful desserts from leftover ingredients at a moment's notice, often making someone's day at the local assisting living home a whole lot yummier and brighter! Sharie's love of anything summer is always as refreshing as this delicious pie.

**Recommended: Flaky Classic Piecrust (page 1)**

### Filling
1 (12-ounce) can pink lemonade concentrate, thawed
2 cups milk
1/2 cup sugar
Dash of salt
1/4 cup plus 1 teaspoon cornstarch, sifted
Zest of 1 lemon
2 teaspoons lemon extract

### Garnish
Sweetie-licious Whipped Cream (double recipe on page 8) with added pink food coloring

1. Mix the pink lemonade, milk, sugar, salt, and cornstarch in a medium pan.

2. Cook on medium heat, stirring constantly until thick and bubbly. Remove from the heat and add the lemon zest and lemon extract.

3. Pour the filling into a piecrust and refrigerate for at least 3 hours.

4. Garnish with Whipped Cream.

# Mom's Comfort Chocolate Chess Pie

## Eat pie, spoil loved ones!

No child wants to be sick, and I was no exception. Being sick meant no play whatsoever—which for us meant no indoor board games, outdoor team games, make-believe, Easy-Bake, Barbies, bike riding, running through the sprinkler, sledding, or skating up the road. When you were sick as a kid back then, there was only one thing good about it—the good eats!

I remember my mother revamping our bedroom for sick stays. She would fluff the pillows with rose-scented pillowcases, lay the Grandmother's Flower Garden quilt at the end of the bed, set up the Vicks Vaporizer in the corner of the room, and place a TV tray next to the bed. The special food she put on the tray was my favorite part of the convalescence period, as it made us feel special too. It might be sassafras tea made with cream and sugar, or a small glass of Vernors ginger ale. But what I remember most fondly were her puddings: creamy rice, brown sugar butterscotch, vanilla, and my cherished chocolate made with Hershey's cocoa, milk, and butter, always chocolaty, warm, creamy, and perfect. It always amazes me how comforting food makes us feel so lovingly content.

**Recommended: Sweetie-licious Cream Cheese Crust, frozen (page 2)**

1. Preheat the oven to 375°F.

2. Line a frozen piecrust with one layer of aluminum foil and fill with one layer of uncooked pasta.

3. Bake in the oven until the bottom of the crust is partially baked, approximately 8 minutes.

4. Carefully lift the pasta-filled foil from the crust.

5. Continue with the directions for the filling below.

**Filling**
1/3 cup cocoa
1 cup sugar
1/2 cup brown sugar
1 1/2 tablespoons flour
1/8 teaspoon salt

2 eggs
1/4 cup butter, melted
1 tablespoon vanilla extract
1 (12-ounce) can evaporated milk
1/2 cup dark chocolate chips

1. Preheat the oven to 375°F.

2. In a large mixing bowl, whisk together the cocoa, sugar, brown sugar, flour, and salt. Set aside.

3. Combine the eggs, butter, and vanilla until well mixed. Add the evaporated milk and mix with a hand mixer. Add the dry ingredients and mix well. Stir in the chocolate chips.

4. Pour into the piecrust and bake for 45 minutes or until the pie is set in the middle.

This pie is over-the-top yummy served with cherry ice cream!

Chapter 8

# LOVE

*"Real love begins where nothing is expected in return."*

*—Antoine de Saint-Exupéry*

Finding love in all things in life is, I believe, truly life's purpose. A heart bursting with love brings happiness to all who encounter it. Love fuels us, and when we find the "loveliness" in everyone, the world is simply sweeter. Hugs, deeds, words, and kind gestures are all expressions of this most powerful virtue.

But baking a pie for someone may be the ultimate testament to love, as the love you bake in it will be crimped into every corner of the crust and suffused in every bite of filling!

# Aunt Margie's Banana Cream Pie

## Eat pie, give love.

My aunt Margie was one of those special people who exuded love in everything she did. All who knew her felt her love and instinctively gave it right back. Life was simply better with Auntie Margie around. When she came to visit, our whole family would anxiously await her arrival. We could hardly wait to see her pull up in her blue Buick packed with gifts for us kids. She routinely brought us chewing gum, comic books, and her famous banana cream pie. Occasionally I would be the lucky one who got to bring the pie in from her car, which was quite a responsibility for a little miss. I remember staring at its perfection and being terrified that I would drop it, knowing that my brothers would never forgive me. Thankfully, the glorious pie always made it into the house unscathed. This is my version of her recipe.

**Recommended: Flaky Classic Piecrust (page 1)**

**Filling**
2 1/2 cups milk
1/2 cup half-and-half
5 egg yolks
1 cup plus 1 teaspoon sugar
1/4 cup plus 1 tablespoon cornstarch, sifted
Dash of salt
1/2 teaspoon vanilla extract
1 1/2 teaspoons banana extract
1 tablespoon butter
3 bananas, yellow, not too ripe

**Garnish—Optional**
Sweetie-licious Whipped Cream (see recipe on page 8)
Dried bananas
Fresh raspberries
White chocolate shavings

"Love is my religion—I could die for it."
—John Keats

1. Preheat the oven to 350°F.

2. Mix the milk, half-and-half, egg yolks, sugar, cornstarch, and salt together in a medium saucepan over medium heat.

3. Stir constantly with a wire whisk until the mixture boils for 1 minute.

4. Remove from the heat. Add the vanilla, banana extract, and butter to the cream mixture.

5. Slice the bananas thinly and arrange the slices in the bottom of a piecrust until it's covered.

6. Pour the cream filling over the banana layer.

7. Cover with plastic wrap and refrigerate for at least 3 hours.

8. Garnish as you wish with Whipped Cream, dried bananas, fresh raspberries, and white chocolate. Best eaten that day.

Cream-based pies should always be refrigerated! They can last up to 3 days in the fridge, but are always best eaten in the first 2 days.

# Grandma Rosella's Vanilla Custard Pie

## Eat pie, open your heart to others.

Back during the bleak Depression, my daddy's cousin Janette came to live with his family for a few special years. Janette's father had seven children when his wife suffered a nervous breakdown and was sent away for treatment. He worked long hours at Ford Motor Company and was unable to care for his children alone. Hence, all seven children were sent separately to live with relatives until the family could get back on its feet. As hard as this was for Janette, the great peace and love she found in my daddy's home influenced her for the rest of her life. Janette recalls how my grandmother Rosella would rock her to sleep, make her new dresses, and bake her vanilla custard pies. These seemingly small acts of kindness were invaluable for a needy, insecure little girl. Janette's family was reunited a few years later, but she says that her favorite childhood memories were with my grandmother, eating pies and feeling loved.

**Recommended: Sweetie-licious Cream Cheese Crust, frozen (page 2)**

1. Preheat the oven to 375°F.
2. Line a frozen piecrust with one layer of aluminum foil and fill with one layer of uncooked pasta.
3. Bake in the oven until the bottom of the crust is partially baked, approximately 8 minutes.
4. Carefully lift the pasta-filled foil from the crust. Let the crust cool.
5. Continue with the directions for the filling below.

**Filling**
1 1/3 cups milk
1 1/2 cups half-and-half
3 egg yolks
3 large eggs
1 cup sugar
1 1/2 tablespoons cornstarch

Dash of salt
1 teaspoon vanilla extract
1/2 teaspoon almond extract
Freshly grated nutmeg

**Garnish—Optional**
Fresh berries

1. Mix the milk, half-and-half, egg yolks, eggs, sugar, cornstarch, and salt together in a medium saucepan over medium heat.

2. Stir constantly with a wire whisk until the mixture just starts to boil. Remove from the heat; add the vanilla and almond extracts.

3. Pour the filling into the piecrust.

4. Grate nutmeg on top of the pie.

5. Bake for 45 minutes or until the center is almost set. Refrigerate for at least 3 hours.

6. Serve with fresh berries, if desired.

My grandma used to make this pie occasionally with raisins or dates during World War II for my father. This pie is wonderful served with fresh fruit in season.

# Grandpa Ferrell's Cherry Rhubarb Pie

Eat pie, love your partner.

My grandpa Ferrell was a coal miner in West Virginia for many years before and after the Depression. Coal miners worked long, dark hours, and often the only bright spot of their day was lunchtime. This was usually one half hour and aboveground, giving them a chance to rest their legs and backs and breathe some clean mountain air. At that time, wives packed lunches in covered tin buckets with the top part of the container designated for dessert, mostly slices of pie. The miners always looked forward to seeing what, if any, kind of pie appeared in their buckets.

The old story went that if a miner had two slices of pie waiting for him in his bucket, then he had made his wife happy and she really loved him. If only one slice was there, the miner was an average husband and his wife cared for him. However, if the bucket's pie tray was empty, that meant that the miner was not making his wife happy and there was no love left! My grandparents were married close to sixty years and needless to say, he had lots of pie. Cherry rhubarb was one of his favorites.

**Recommended: Flaky Classic Piecrust, frozen (page 1), Sweetie-licious Crumb Topping (page 6)**

### Filling
1 cup plus 2 tablespoons sugar
1/4 cup cornstarch, sifted
6 cups frozen unsweetened pitted
   Michigan tart red cherries

1/8 teaspoon orange zest
1/8 teaspoon almond extract
2 1/2 cups fresh or frozen rhubarb (if using
   fresh, cut in 1/2-inch slices)

1. Preheat the oven to 375°F.

2. Combine the sugar, cornstarch, cherries, and orange zest in a medium pan.

3. Cook on medium heat, stirring constantly until thickened.

4. Add the almond extract and fresh or frozen rhubarb.

5. Pour the filling into a frozen piecrust.

6. Cover with Crumb Topping, covering all of the pie filling.

7. Bake for 1 hour or more, or until the pie filling bubbles over.

8. Cool on a rack and keep at room temperature.

# Mrs. Pricco's Fresh Strawberry Rhubarb Pie

Eat pie, share your time.

My friend Mrs. Pricco was one endearing woman. She was full of fun and had a smile that lit up a room and warmed your heart. She always was doing lovely things for other people—taking older relatives to church and doctor appointments, and making delicious meals and desserts for the downhearted and lonely. She simply loved to make someone's average day a wonderful one. Mrs. Pricco's homemade fresh strawberry rhubarb pies were loved by everyone who received one, especially by her adoring family. She was indeed a woman we should all emulate. She lived her life simply and beautifully, giving to others her time, her laughter, and her love.

**Recommended: Flaky Classic Piecrust, frozen (page 1), Sweetie-licious Crumb Topping (page 6)**

**Filling**
1 1/4 cups sugar
1/4 cup plus 1 tablespoon tapioca (minute variety)
4 cups washed, hulled, and sliced fresh strawberries
2 cups diced fresh rhubarb, cut in 1/2-inch chunks
1 teaspoon fresh lime juice
1/2 teaspoon fresh orange zest

> "Love is the beginning, the middle and the end of everything."
> —Lacordaire

1. Preheat the oven to 375°F.

2. Mix the sugar, tapioca, strawberries, rhubarb, lime juice, and orange zest in a large bowl for 10 minutes or until the tapioca softens. Do not let the mixture stand too long or it will become too juicy to thicken properly.

3. Pour the filling in a frozen piecrust. Cover with Crumb Topping, covering all of the pie filling.

4. Bake for an hour or more, or until the pie filling bubbles over and a knife slides easily into the middle of the pie.

5. Cool on a rack and keep at room temperature. Best eaten on the first day.

## Favorite Pie

I am often asked if I have a favorite pie, and I truthfully cannot pick just one. It is indeed like asking if you have a favorite son or daughter; you simply cannot choose! Still, I enjoy seasonal pies the very best. I have always loved the change in seasons, and enjoy decorating my farmette and the shop to celebrate the different times of year and holidays. And I love seasonal cooking and baking to complement them as well, especially pies!

In the spring I absolutely adore rhubarb pies. The sweet-tart fruit filling paired with a buttery crust is truly unbeatable. This is our family's all-time favorite pie for May birthdays and Memorial Day picnics.

Come early summer I cannot wait to have a strawberry and cream pie with fresh-picked sweet strawberries set atop creamy vanilla custard filling. Later in the summer I adore fresh blueberry and peach pies, and love combining the two for pure summer love. Eating slices of these pies on my front porch is a summer must!

Once my favorite season of fall arrives, I cannot wait for caramel apple and pumpkin pies. I love how they taste exactly like crisp autumn, and both are a staple at our Harvest Home barn party.

As for winter, I adore pecan pie for holiday entertaining and love butterscotch praline for winter Sunday dinners. Both are rich and deep with flavor—perfect to warm your soul in the coldest season!

*Eat pie, love life.*

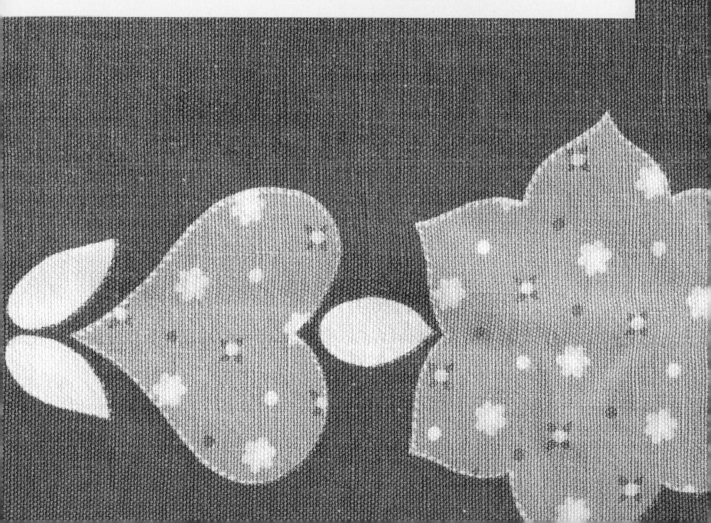

# Mr. Brickley's Lemon Pecan Chess Pie

## Eat pie, love life!

Mr. Brickley, a dear family friend, had a delightful old home that smelled of fragrant pipe tobacco and roses. It also had a unique sound, as dozens of antique clocks chimed melodious tunes throughout the large house. A favorite of our family, he was a great storyteller. During one of my last visits with him, I asked him if he had a favorite pie. Confined to his bed, he smiled as he spoke of a lemon nut pie his mother used to bake. I hurried home and searched through my vintage recipes to find a baked lemon chess pie recipe. I knew cancer could weaken taste buds, so I added extra quantities of fresh lemon juice and pecans to his pie and brought it on my next visit.

When I fed him his first bite, a small tear ran down his sweet, aged face, as he said he hadn't tasted "his mother's pie" for eighty years! I made the pie for him for three more weeks, as it was came to be the only thing he could eat. The nurse later told me he died after his last bite of "mother's lemon pie" while recalling his happy boyhood days during the 1900s. It wasn't long after that experience that I decided I had to make pies for a living.

Mr. Brickley and his pie led me to understand the true healing power of food, and especially pies, to a person's soul. Pies can transport folks back home to Mother, to the warmth of her hugs and kitchen stove, to a simpler time of love, innocence, and childhood.

**Recommended: Flaky Classic Piecrust, frozen (page 1)**

1. Preheat the oven to 375°F.
2. Line a frozen piecrust with one layer of aluminum foil and fill with one layer of uncooked pasta.
3. Bake in the oven until the bottom of the crust is partially baked, approximately 8 minutes.
4. Carefully lift the pasta-filled foil from the crust. Let the crust cool.
5. Continue with the directions for the filling below.

### Filling

1/4 cup butter, melted
1 1/2 cups brown sugar
1/8 teaspoon salt
3 eggs
1 1/2 tablespoons flour
1/2 cup heavy cream
3/4 cup chopped pecans, toasted
Zest of 2 lemons
Juice of 2 lemons

1. Preheat the oven to 375°F.

2. In a large bowl, combine the butter, brown sugar, salt, and eggs. Mix by hand until the ingredients are combined.

3. Add the flour, cream, pecans, lemon zest, and lemon juice. Continue to mix by hand until the ingredients are well mixed.

4. Pour into the piecrust and bake for 45–50 minutes, or until the pie is set in the middle.

### Lemon Glaze

1/4 cup confectioners' sugar
Zest of 1/2 lemon
1 tablespoon freshly squeezed lemon juice
1/4 teaspoon lemon extract
1/4 cup pecans, toasted and chopped

1. Mix the confectioners' sugar, lemon zest, lemon juice, and lemon extract in a medium bowl with a whisk until smooth.

2. While the pie is still warm, drizzle lemon glaze over its entire surface. Sprinkle with chopped pecans.

 Chess and nut pies freeze very well.

"Nothing, nothing
compares to the loveliness of
love. Give all to love. . . ."
—Ralph Waldo Emerson

# Mom McComb's Mocha Hot Chocolate Pie

## Eat pie, serve love in all you do!

Growing up in Michigan, we enjoyed plenty of snowy days and all the fun activities that went along with them. Ice skating was a family favorite. The park at the end of our street was transformed into an ice rink in the winter, complete with a warming house, outdoor lights, and music underneath large sycamore trees. After school my siblings and I would race home, put on our ice skates, and skate down the ice-covered street to the rink. We would meet our friends there to play crack the whip, pretend to be Dorothy Hamill, and ice dance to the music all afternoon.

On Saturdays, after a full day of skating and numb from the cold, we would anxiously skate home, hoping to be met not only by the warmth of the house, but also by the fragrant smell of chocolate. My mother's steaming, rich hot chocolate was extra special, made with cream, cinnamon, and a splash of her leftover morning coffee, topped by a large marshmallow and served in antique teacups and saucers. I remember our little hands wrapped around our cups, tipping the marshmallow into the pond of chocolate bliss with our tongues. I hope you feel the same sense of love while enjoying this most delicious, cold version created as a pie!

**Recommended: Flaky Classic Piecrust (page 1)**

1. Preheat the oven to 375°F.

2. Line a frozen piecrust with one layer of aluminum foil and fill with one layer of uncooked pasta.

3. Bake in the oven until the bottom of the crust is light brown, approximately 25 minutes.

4. Carefully lift the foil from the crust. Let the crust cool.

### Filling
2¹/₂ cups whole milk
¹/₂ cup half-and-half
1¹/₄ cups sugar
4 egg yolks
¹/₃ cup cornstarch, sifted
¹/₃ cup Hershey's cocoa, sifted
¹/₂ teaspoon coffee extract OR 1 rounded tablespoon finely ground espresso powder
¹/₄ teaspoon vanilla extract

### Garnish—Optional
Sweetie-licious Whipped Cream (see recipe on page 8)
Marshmallow cream
Marshmallows
Chocolate shavings or syrup

1. Mix the milk, half-and-half, sugar, and egg yolks in a medium pan.

2. Sift together the cornstarch, cocoa, and espresso powder, if using; add to the pan.

3. Cook on medium heat, stirring constantly until the mixture thickens. Remove from the heat.

4. Add the vanilla extract and coffee extract, if using.

5. Pour the filling into a piecrust, cover with plastic wrap, and refrigerate for at least 3 hours.

6. Garnish with Whipped Cream, drizzled marshmallow cream or marshmallows, and chocolate shavings.

Melinda's
Rhubarb Pie

CHALLENGE

'09 Best of Show Winne

108 N. Bridge St. DeWi

48820 517-669-9300 sweetie-licious.com

# ACKNOWLEDGMENTS
## Thank you, thank you, thank you—

To my foremothers, whose human spirit was ignited by character, faith, gratitude, joy, work ethic, passion, kindness, and love, and for sharing these virtues through their pies!

To my sweet parents—for my mommy's pie legacy and my daddy's love of pie!

Mom Hundt—showing the great love that goes into baking every day.

To my beloved twin sister, Laura, my very first baking partner, who showed me the fun of baking since our Easy-Bake Oven days! And to my brothers, Mark, Paul, and David, for loving everything we made!

Melinda Hundt, my first believer, and professional pie baker partner!

To all of my co-workers at Sweetie-licious, who also happen to be my best friends. They exude virtues of hard work, passion, and love with each customer and in everything they bake everyday at the shop. Especially, my inspiring fellow bakers who helped develop these recipes and made them beautiful for this cookbook—Stephanie Haynie, Sharie Curtin, Patty Blackmond, Eileen Hundt, and Gretchen Karslake. And to Cheryl Kellogg for her loyal dedication of following me around the shop for years, writing down the recipes as I created them.

To my dear friend, Jeannie Cleary, for all of her tireless work to make this cookbook a reality.

To Kim Schram, for being my BFF/Business Partner and getting this dream cookbook off the ground!

Gail Junion Metz, Jenn Wagoner, and Sue Rundborg for their creative talents to make this cookbook as beautiful as it is.

To all the gracious recipe testers that helped perfect these delicious pies for everyone!

To my photographer, Clarissa, and the team at the Kalman & Pabst Photo Group, and food stylist, Laura Goble, for creating breath-taking pictures of not only pies, but a lifestyle!

To Elizabeth Evans, from Jean Naggar Agency, and Mary Norris and the team from skirt!/Globe Pequot, for believing in me and the love of pie. I am tickled pink that it is as beautiful as we envisioned it! I am forever grateful.

To my kind and loyal customers, my Facebook fans, Twitter followers, webpage/blog followers, and all of my sweet friends and family that have supported me and Sweetie-licious pies since I starting selling them from my back porch years ago!

To my dear husband, John, and our lovely daughters, Ellie and Betsie—I cannot thank you enough for all of your love and support to make this "pie dream" come true. You are my favorite people on this earth, and I am blessed to share my life and pies with each of you! My love always.

To God, who believed in me, and that my love for people and pie baking could help change the world one pie at a time!

# METRIC CONVERSION CHART

## Metric U.S. Approximate Equivalents

**Liquid Ingredients**

| METRIC | U.S. MEASURES | METRIC | U.S. MEASURES |
|--------|---------------|--------|---------------|
| 1.23 ML | 1/4 TSP. | 29.57 ML | 2 TBSP. |
| 2.36 ML | 1/2 TSP. | 44.36 ML | 3 TBSP. |
| 3.70 ML | 3/4 TSP. | 59.15 ML | 1/4 CUP |
| 4.93 ML | 1 TSP. | 118.30 ML | 1/2 CUP |
| 6.16 ML | 1 1/4 TSP. | 236.59 ML | 1 CUP |
| 7.39 ML | 1 1/2 TSP. | 473.18 ML | 2 CUPS OR 1 PT. |
| 8.63 ML | 1 3/4 TSP. | 709.77 ML | 3 CUPS |
| 9.86 ML | 2 TSP. | 946.36 ML | 4 CUPS OR 1 QT. |
| 14.79 ML | 1 TBSP. | 3.79 L | 4 QTS. OR 1 GAL. |

**Dry Ingredients**

| METRIC | U.S. MEASURES | METRIC | U.S. MEASURES | |
|--------|---------------|--------|---------------|---|
| 2 (1.8) G | 1/16 OZ. | 80 G | 2 4/5 OZ. | |
| 31/2 (3.5) G | 1/8 OZ. | 85 (84.9) G | 3 OZ. | |
| 7 (7.1) G | 1/4 OZ. | 100 G | 3 1/2 OZ. | |
| 15 (14.2) G | 1/2 OZ. | 115 (113.2) G | 4 OZ. | |
| 21 (21.3) G | 3/4 OZ. | 125 G | 4 1/2 OZ. | |
| 25 G | 7/8 OZ. | 150 G | 5 1/4 OZ. | |
| 30 (28.3) G | 1 OZ. | 250 G | 8 7/8 OZ. | |
| 50 G | 1 3/4 OZ. | 454 G | 1 LB. | 16 OZ. |
| 60 (56.6) G | 2 OZ. | 500 G | 1 LIVRE | 17 3/5 OZ. |

# INDEX

# ABOUT THE AUTHOR

Linda Hundt is a sixteen-time national pie-baking champion, including two Bests in Show. She has been featured on the Food Network and other television programs, in newspaper and magazine articles throughout the country, and as a guest columnist for various Michigan publications. Sweetie-licious Bakery Café and Linda have won numerous baking, restaurant, and business awards, including the Crisco 100 Year Anniversary Innovation Award and the Food Network Amazing Pie Challenge.

Linda is a true believer that delicious memories make the world a more meaningful, joyous, and loving place. She is the proprietor of Sweetie-licious Bakery Café, the cutest little pie shop in the whole wide world, and believes that loving people and making delicious pies is her mission in life. Linda lives on a farm in DeWitt, Michigan, and is the mother of two charming and beautiful grown daughters and the wife of an equally charming and beautiful husband of over twenty-eight years.

Visit her at sweetie-licious.com, on Twitter @sweetie-licious, or on Facebook Sweetie-licious Bakery Café.